Unbreakable Bonds

by

Elnora Wood Crane

CRANE PUBLISHING
INDIANAPOLIS

First Edition - Large Print

ISBN 0-9741053-0-9

Printed in the United States of America

IN MEMORY OF

my parents
Ruth and Victor Wood
and
Aunt Mildred and Uncle Albert Beck
for sharing their home and lives with us.
We all shall be indebted to them with our love.

ACKNOWLEDGMENTS

This book never would have been written without my loving, patient, untiring family. There have been many drafts of the book written and rewritten. I have received many well accepted corrective statements as well as much encouragement.

My thanks to my brothers, sisters, and cousins for their contributions to this book.

My thanks to my loving husband, Bob, and my daughter, Londa, for allowing me to escape to the quiet world of writing.

Lastly, my thanks to Nancy Kidd for her technical support.

TABLE OF CONTENTS

CHAPTER

1

Our Mother and Father

Mark 10:14

*Suffer the little children to come unto Me,
and forbid them not:
for of such is the Kingdom of God.*

Mom (Ruth Wood)   *Dad (August Wood)*
                        and Katherine

Our life began like any other family living on Missouri Street in Indianapolis, Indiana. We had a loving mother and father, Ruth and August Wood. Our mother was a small-framed person. Mom was very pretty and looked like a princess that had come to life. She was slightly crippled from polio that she had contracted as a child. As a result of the polio, she lost the use of one of her lungs. Our father was a tall, slender, good-looking man. There were six of us, and we attended church every Sunday, where our father was the preacher. The three youngest children--Jim, Leon, and Norie--would ride in an old buggy, while Katherine, Mildred and George had to walk with Mom and Dad. Of course, I was too young to remember that. I am Elnora (Norie), the baby of the family. (I always remind my brothers and sisters of that.)

Life on Missouri Street was good. The house we lived in had three rooms and all eight of us slept in one bedroom. Dad spread paste wax on the living room's old linoleum floor, then covered two or three bricks in old pieces of blankets. The older kids sat on the floor, sliding the bricks back and forth, with Dad in the middle making it a big game. When they were done, the floor shined like a silver dollar in a mud hole. The kids did not realize they were polishing the floor.

The older children remember listening to "The Hermit's Cave" and other scary stories on the radio once a week. As we listened, we were terrified and loved it! By the end of the program, everyone was sitting either on Dad's lap or on the floor beside him. There we felt safe.

One day Mil decided she wanted to stay home from school with Mom. She took

3

one of her only pair of shoes and threw it in the top of the closet. By the end of the day Dad decided he was definitely going to find that shoe. Well, he found it and she never pulled that stunt again!

Mil was the most helpful and desirable student a teacher could ever ask for. She and a friend decided they would do a favor for their teacher, Miss Myers, and polish her new car. They took newspapers and buffed it real well. Proudly they told her about the job they had done and took her outside to see her new car. She made a visible effort to be kind and friendly, but the look of horror on her face showed them something was wrong. They had scratched the car all to pieces!

On another occasion, Kat's teacher, Ms. Stone, knew we were a poor family. She took Kat out and bought her a complete outfit and a new coat. This was because she knew Kat had so many responsibilities at home. Many years after Kat was grown and had children of her own, she applied for a job at an insurance company. The employer's name was Stone. She told him, "I used to have a teacher by the name of Stone at School #12." He said, "That was my daughter!"

Kat was very sickly and pale when she was very young. She was put in a class called the "fresh air room". Each morning all the children in this program were given a hot bowl of oatmeal. Then in the afternoon they were given graham crackers and milk. I guess this was intended to put meat on their bones and color in their faces.

Dad was a handyman of sorts and worked at a warehouse all day. When he came home he was always busy with first one thing then another. The widow lady next door seemed to know every move made at our place. One day she caught Mil and Kat swinging on the screen door having a high-o' time. She screamed at them, "Get off that door! That will be something else for your dad to fix when he gets home." They responded, "It's none of your business, we can do what we want!"

Well, she repeated their words to Dad. He marched them over there and made them apologize. She knew Dad and his ways so she had expected them and had a tray of cookies for them to take home. Dad seldom spanked his children, and we didn't want to hear his pep talks too often. To repair each wrong deed, he marched us to whomever

5

and made us apologize. That usually hurt more than a spanking.

Mom was a dedicated mother and she always had freshly baked cookies when we came home from school. When she became too ill to bake, from her sick bed she taught Kat to bake. When Mom became bedridden, the city sent help to our house. One lady in particular sticks in the minds of the older children. She was a beautiful black woman and she loved our family. We always liked to see her come and make sweet potato pie for us.

Friday was the big night to go shopping at our house. We went to Leonard's corner store. Mr. Leonard was a swell old man. Mom ran a tab all week and on Fridays Dad went to pay it off.

Mr. Leonard always gave Mil and Kat a sack of penny candies. One day Mom sent the two of them to the store. They were strolling along the sidewalk, each eating her one piece of penny candy. When they walked in the house, Dad gave them a stern look and said, "Where did you get that?" and they answered, "Mr. Leonard gave it to us." Dad asked, "Are you sure?" Mil stuck to her guns but Kat, with her lip quivering, began to cry, "No, Daddy, we stole it." Dad pulled himself out of the chair and said, "That's just what I thought." He switched both of them all the way to Leonard's store and made them apologize.

After she was grown, Mil stopped by to see Mr. Leonard and he told her, "After your mother died and you kids went to live with your aunt, your Dad was one lost soul. He used to come in here and cry his heart out, saying he did not want to live anymore."

Only one Christmas sticks in the minds of the older Wood children. That year Mil and Kat each received a Shirley Temple doll. One had a red polka dot dress and the other one had a blue polka dot dress. The boys got BB guns, but after Jim accidentally shot our baby brother Leon in the lip, Dad took all of the guns and wrapped them around a tree.

The day Mom died the girls knew they were leaving to go to Aunt Mil's house. They put their dolls in Mom's cedar chest for safekeeping, never to be seen again. Writing about this brings a tear to my eye even now.

When I was eighteen months old, Mother came down with dropsy, which led to double pneumonia, and she died. This was before penicillin was available. Mom died on Mother's Day in 1942, at the age of thirty-four. Her death turned our lives upside down.

Mom and Jim

My mother and Aunt Mil, who was my father's sister, were best of friends. My mother, knowing she had contracted pneumonia and had use of only one lung, asked Aunt Mil to take care of her babies if she died.

After my mother's death, our father turned to the bottle and developed a serious drinking problem. He had lost his wife and was unable to manage six kids on his own. The end result is that we were turned over to his sister Mildred and her husband, Albert Beck. Aunt Mil was keeping her promise to my mother and taking care of her children.

Aunt Mil was a matronly type woman who wore her hair in braids on top of her head. She was a stay-at-home mother all her years. She never drove a car and was content without it. Uncle Al never tired of driving her around; however, that was not uncommon in those days.

Top: Katherine and Mil
Bottom: George and Jim

Back: Mom, Kat, and Dad
Front: Jim, Mil, and George

CHAPTER

2

Life on the Farm

Proverbs 22:6

Train a child in the way he should go,
and when he is old
he will not turn from it.

Chapter 2

Arvine, Uncle Al, and Aunt Mil Beck

Aunt Mil and Uncle Al were married ten years before they had their only child, a son. Arvine was a cute boy with a powder white baby face and he always had a smile on his face.

Both Aunt Mil and Uncle Al grew up in orphanages. Aunt Mil was content with her life in a Catholic home; she was treated well and taken good care of. Uncle Al's youth was quite different. He was born in Texas, and had three brothers. When he was young, the family left Texas in a covered wagon and headed north, where the boys were placed in a children's home in Fort Wayne, Indiana. The children were terribly mistreated, beaten, and made to work extremely hard. One of the brothers was adopted from the home and Uncle Al never saw or heard from him again. When he turned 18, Uncle Al left the home, got a job, and eventually took in his other two brothers.

We always will be grateful to Aunt Mil and Uncle Al for taking all of us in, and for their love and generosity. Their impact on our lives is indelible.

Unquestionably, life was tough in our new surroundings but Dad came down and visited us often. When he arrived he would be crying, and when he left to go home he would be crying. Of course, that made the whole crew cry. This went on the whole time we lived there. His hands were tied and he never knew which way to turn. We each had our own separate fears to work through.

Aunt Mil and Uncle Al owned a grocery store in Indianapolis, and traded it for a small farm, as we called it, consisting of seven acres, three-and-a-half miles southeast of Cloverdale, Indiana. It was just south of Tile Factory Road, and one-half mile off County Line Road on Millgrove Road. Liefel Goss was the previous owner.

Cloverdale was a small, rural farming town with a population of approximately 1,600 at that time.

The farm consisted of a house with three rooms: one bedroom, a living room, and a kitchen. There was an attic but it wasn't finished and seldom was used. In reality it was a tiny shack. It was a gloomy old house but it was our new home.

Mil and Ed (inset) at our old farm house

There was no running water or electricity and the only lights we had came from kerosene lamps, which meant constantly cleaning the globes. Electricity came much later and we had great fun with it when it was hooked up to the outhouse. In the winter it was hard to touch our feet to the cold floor before someone stoked the wood stove.

Uncle Al bought an old horse named George, but we had enough Georges in our family so he renamed him Charlie. Whenever one of us called out "Charlie!", the poor horse was so confused, he looked

Arvine, Jim, Charlie, Uncle Al, George, Vic

the other way. Charlie never had been ridden before so the boys rode him bareback. Uncle Al purchased him rather cheaply and since Charlie wasn't really good for much, the price was right. I think he was sneaking into the locoweed, too, since all he wanted to do was bite the boys.

The farm had a gravel lane to the main road, rolling hills, beautiful oak trees, walnut trees, grapevines, an old graveyard, and an outhouse. All of us--Kat, Mil, George, Jim, Leon and Norie--moved to the farm with the Beck family.

Everyone had his or her own chores to do. I was exempt because I was too young. Kat, 14, and Mil, 12, got the worst of it because they were older. Chores were endless for them. The day started early with the girls getting ready for school, then making sure everyone had their lunches packed and looked presentable.

The school we attended was a very small brick structure and the Woods made up a good part of the student body. Most of the grades met together in one huge room.

Aunt Mil insisted Mil and Kat wear long, ugly socks with oxford shoes. Oh, how they hated those socks! Off the whole crew would go, walking down the long lane to catch the school bus. The girls walked briskly until they were out of sight and then they changed their socks. They could not go to school in those awful socks, so they had their friends bring more acceptable ones.

Mil knew how to push Aunt Mil's buttons and before leaving for school one day, she said, "Someday when I am grown I will be rich and I won't have to wear these ugly socks."

Their skirts were extra long and unstylish so they rolled them up at the waistband several times until they were shorter and looked more like the other girls' skirts. Finally they added a little lipstick, which was a sin in our Pentecostal household.

At the end of the school day, they got off the bus and put their ugly socks back on and then took their time walking back down the lane for another long night of work. They decided on the walks back which chores each would take. Homework was done only if there was time. The younger children had to be bathed, and there was dinner to cook and beds to make. Aunt Mil supervised, but I cannot remember her actually doing much of the work. I did not attend school at that time because I was too young.

Aunt Mil's expectations were high, and sometimes destructive. Out of fear of rejection, we had to walk the straight and narrow.

Chapter 2

There were fields behind the house, and when I was very young Aunt Mil would say, "Look, Norie, there's a hobo in the field. He's coming to the door to beg for food." I would run to the window peering through the glass looking for the hobo. Aunt Mil would say, "Let's go take a nap and he'll think we're not home." With my heart pounding, I would run and jump in the bed, covering my head, so the hobo wouldn't see me. As I got older, I realized Aunt Mil's purpose in telling me about the hobo was to get me to take a nap. There was never a hobo, just hunters in the fields.

We laugh now about the belt she always carried around her neck. It was to scare us, I think, and it did a pretty good job. She had to keep some kind of control with seven kids running around. She called the belt "The Persuader". Aunt Mil definitely spread the Gospel with her discipline if someone did something she thought was wrong. She kept a chart with black marks for each person. I am not sure what would have happened when the list was full, but no one wanted to find out.

Of the three boys, George was the oldest, very thin, and pale. Jim was next, and a very good-looking boy. Then there was the youngest, Leon, and he was very shy. They each had many chores as well. They had buckets and were to keep the water supply coming into the house. Jim said he often thought his middle name was "Get Water". Sometimes one or the other would hide out in the "glorious" outhouse and read the Sears catalog to avoid carrying water. When they were caught, they usually got extra chores. Our life was good though, because we were surviving and the six of us all stayed together.

The shed and the outhouse

Uncle George, Uncle Ed, and Dad

CHAPTER

3

Cousins Join the Family

Psalms 27:10

When my Father and Mother forsake me,
Then the Lord will take me up.

After living in Cloverdale for a year, some of our cousins came to live with us in our small three-room farmhouse. Aunt Mil's brothers had family problems for one reason or another and could not care for their children. Aunt Mil and Uncle Al took them in.

First it was her brother George's children, Victor and Joan. Vic had sparkling eyes that seemed to peer right through you and always had a smile. Joan had olive skin and dark hair. Aunt Mil's brother George had married a crippled lady, and when he was drafted in 1942, she could not, or did not want, to care for Vic and Joan while he was away. Their mother was not in the picture at this time in their lives. Aunt Mil was made their guardian. Joan refused to go to Aunt Mil's unless she could take her nanny goat, Roseanne, with her.

Next to join our extended family were Aunt Mil's brother Edward's five children. They were Ed, John, Hattie, Paul, and Ella. Ed looked like his Indian heritage and was very mischievous. He sure knew how to push Aunt Mil's buttons. He held his head to one side because of tight tendons in his neck. John was good looking and could charm a statue with his personality. Hattie was a chubby little girl who liked to eat. Paul always wanted to be a preacher and Ella was very talented musically.

Uncle Edward had a drinking problem like our father. Their mother took them to the Children's Guardian Home in Indianapolis, and said, "Here they are. I cannot care for them." Aunt Mil got word of this and went to the Home and took them to the farm. The count was now up to fourteen children.

When Aunt Mil came home and told everyone what she had done, Katherine, being the oldest and carrying the most responsibility, put her hands on her hips and stated, "Well, I think we have enough work to do already." That was a mistake and she got smacked across the mouth. Aunt Mil and Uncle Al had big hearts and if someone asked them to do something, they could not say no.

We were definitely in close quarters with fourteen kids plus two adults living in our three-room house. For us kids, it was great fun having a huge extended family. Our cousins quickly became our brothers and sisters. There were no fights or jealousy. We were all in the same boat--we needed a place to live. There was never a dull moment. What one did not think of another one did.

There were four beds and a couch in the living room. We slept four to a bed and some slept crosswise. We tied our shoelaces together when we went to bed so all those shoes wouldn't get mixed up and there would be no frantic searches for the mates in the morning. Aunt Mil, Uncle Al, and Arvine slept in the bedroom.

I am not sure where all our clothes and coats came from. There never seemed to be a problem. Some of our coats were put together from many scrap fabrics and were so colorful they looked like Joseph's coat of many colors, but they kept us warm. Boots were unheard of but you don't miss what you don't have.

Our memories of Christmas are few. The boys, with the help of Uncle Al, went out and cut down a tree, brought it in, and hoped they could get it to stand straight. There were no presents due to lack of money so Christmas was just another day. Rarely we got oranges, apples, and nuts.

The kids used a big needle to string popcorn and cranberries to make garlands. Boy did we ever have the garlands when everyone got busy! They cut colored construction paper in strips to make chains. This served two purposes: it kept them busy and filled their time, but it also gave us our only Christmas tree decorations. Our life was good because we were surviving and the six of us all stayed together.

We ate in double shifts, first the kids, then the adults. We had to wash the dishes between shifts because we did not have enough for everyone. We sat at a large table that had a bench on each side and a chair at each end. Uncle Ed said there were so many mouths to feed that he could toss up a loaf of bread in the air and every slice would be gone before it hit the table!

Jowl bacon was always on hand. We had it for breakfast and Aunt Mil also put it in beans. Spam and Treet were always welcomed meats. There was nothing like a treat of fried Spam and fried potatoes. We went through many a bag of rice, too; it was used for breakfast with cinnamon, sugar and milk added.

Aunt Mil made pies on deep cookie sheets. Our favorites were blackberry cobblers that were made from berries we picked in five-gallon buckets. It was always nice when the windows were open and a

25

breeze spread the sweet scent of her yeast bread. Aunt Mil made all the jelly and sealed the tops with paraffin. Flapjacks were always good. They were made of biscuit dough and were fried in deep fat.

When we had potato soup, Aunt Mil drafted the whole clan into peeling the potatoes. She made a mean vegetable soup and any gust of wind would blow the aroma to the next farm. She used a seven-quart kettle for the soup one day and then for beans on the other days. One has not lived until one has lived in a three-room house with sixteen people eating beans two or three days a week!

We raised chickens and collected eggs. Aunt Mil caught the chickens, wrung their necks, and then they flip-flopped all over the ground. Then she put them in a pot of boiling water and plucked their feathers. If I had to do that today, I never would eat chicken.

When Uncle George came home on furlough from the Army, his first stop was the farm to visit his children. He told Aunt Mil he was hungry for fried chicken. She told him, "Honey, you're my baby brother. You go out and kill as many chickens as you want and we'll have fried chicken." Uncle

George stood there shuffling his feet and then went out and killed twenty-four chickens! We had enough chicken for the whole county. He took fried chicken home with him on the train. When Uncle Al returned home and heard about the chicken kill, it was very difficult for him to hold his tongue, but he did a nice job of it. I am sure he had many thoughts churning in his brain. It certainly depleted our egg supply. Some of us loved Uncle George's trick though because it meant a few people would get new pillows. Aunt Mil always took the chicken feathers to make pillows. It was a toss up to see who would get the new pillows.

We had an arrogant rooster who seemed to want to rule the roost. All night long he would crow, and all day he would chase the kids around to show his authority. He was determined to destroy anyone in his path, or anyone he could.

Uncle Al once found two baby crows that had fallen from their nest and soon they were part of our family. We raised them on boiled eggs. They liked to follow everyone around and often they hitched a ride on the nearest person's shoulder. One day one of the crows came up missing, only to be found drowned in the rain barrel. The boys buried him in the backyard and planted a cross at the grave.

After Joan and Vic arrived with their goat Roseanne, Uncle Al bought a billy goat. Before long, we had baby goats running all around bucking everyone they could find in the seat of the pants. They liked to get on top of the house and into Uncle Al's new trees. One day someone left the door of his pickup truck open, and thanks to the goats, the seats were gone in no time.

School was never the same once the Wood crew hit the area. Word circulated fast throughout the school that the Wood kids had arrived. I am sure it rocked the whole community. The boys looked out for each other. Each was adventurous and had his own turf on which to trod. On Vic's report card, the principal wrote, "Contrary to popular belief, the Wood boys do *not* run the Cloverdale School."

Chores doubled when the cousins came to live with us. In the summer there was always a garden with vegetables to be prepared for canning. Most were green beans, corn and tomatoes. Corn was a main grain on our table; seldom did we have a meal without hominy, grits or cornbread. The vegetables were canned by the cold packing method, and canned goods were stored in the fruit cellar. It was fun to go down there to see all the dusty old jars lined up neatly on the shelves.

From time to time, the cellar filled up with water and Uncle Al worked with the boys to pump it out. Almost all our food was produced in our yard, fields, or garden. Uncle Al taught my brothers to hunt for mushrooms, and they still love to go mushroom hunting today.

Saturday was washday. First the girls stomped the clothes clean in the washtub with lye soap. Mil always read comic books on the sly while stomping the clothes. When she heard Aunt Mil coming, she would toss the comic books and stomp double-time. Next they graduated to a scrub board, which made the scent of the lye soap even more evident, but they really got a break when Uncle Al bought a wringer washer.

Joan's job was to wash the hankies everyone used during the week. There were no such things as Kleenex or paper towels in those days. Everything went through that wringer at least three times. Sometimes a few became entangled in the wringer, going around and around, and had to be pulled out manually.

Next it was time for the heavy, heaping baskets of sheets and towels to be pulled to the clothesline. Once there, it was time for the clothespin bag fight. They pinned the clothespins to their collars and sleeves, and stuffed their mouths full for easy reach.

A few hours later it was time to retrieve the clothes, so back to the line for folding practice. Afterwards, Aunt Mil told the boys to bring the folded clothes into the house. The girls knew the boys were coming when they heard the squeaky wheel of the wheelbarrow. The boys came flying around the corner with one riding and one pushing. They loaded the wheelbarrow with the newly folded clothes and took them inside.

In the rainy season, we used the water in the cistern to wash clothes. If we had a dry spell, the boys had to hit the water trail double-time and carry more water. Ed had so much energy that he was always three steps ahead of the others.

The outhouse had to be moved every six months and the boys had to dig the new hole each time. It seemed like we were forever moving the outhouse with that many people. The big problem at night was remembering which direction to go!

Ed and George

There were no favorites; everyone was an equal. I am convinced this helped to mold us into the people we are today. We all had one common goal--survival.

One day Aunt Mil got fed up and told Uncle Al, "I can't get those girls to do anything, Albert. You are going to have to straighten them out." He said, "All right, enough is enough," giving them a slight wink. "You girls get in the bedroom and lie across the bed." There were Mil, Kat, and Hattie lying on the bed. He came in, closed the door, and gave each one a pillow. "Put this on your bottom, and when I hit the pillow, you holler and cry." Boy, did they ever turn it on. They screamed and cried as though they were choking on their own sobs. That was their secret whipping. I don't know if Aunt Mil ever found out they were all bluffing.

Leon was four years old when our mother died. He had a bed-wetting problem and Aunt Mil punished him by rubbing his nose in the wet sheets. They woke him in the middle of the night trying to get him to go to the bathroom. If he could not, they poured cold water over his penis. If that did not work, they put him on the attic stairs and told him the rats were coming. My sister Mil recently asked Leon if he remembers that and he said he recalls her whispering to him, "I'm here, don't be afraid. There are no rats." When they let him out, his little eyes were wet and shiny. His sobs still stab at our hearts today.

He also had a stuttering problem and they always made fun of him. He was such a cute boy and did nothing to deserve such treatment. To this day, I don't understand why they chose to pick on him the way they did.

Leon

Aunt Mil especially liked to get my sister Mil riled up since Mil had a temper when she was upset. Aunt Mil held her down and let someone take a whack at her, just to torment her. She would come up fighting and run to the graveyard with her guitar, where she would play and sing to cool off. Aunt Mil meant well, but I don't think she really knew how to handle that many homeless children.

Aunt Mil's sister Edna had a son named Frank Tooley. Frank was our first cousin also, but one Aunt Mil didn't take in to raise. Frank was a woman charmer and he loved his drinks. He was lost in the sauce and killed at the age of thirty in a car accident. Frank did one thing in his life that was great: he served his country in the Navy.

Jane and Wanda were schoolmates of Mil and Kat, as well as neighbors. They had the type of smile that seemed to draw smiles in return. They came down the lane to play with Mil and Kat, but there were always chores to be done, so Jane and Wanda chipped in to help. They formed a club called "The Four Hicks from the Sticks." The club got together to make and eat fudge, which they usually ended up eating with a spoon.

Mil and Wanda

Mil and Wanda always wanted to spend a lot of time together but got themselves into trouble. For example, Ernie was their school bus driver whom they liked a lot. One day they hid in the school basement so they would miss the bus. They watched out the basement window, giggling, while Ernie waited for them, but finally, with a puzzled look on his face, he drove off without them. They got what they wanted, more time together--to walk three miles home in the snow! Wanda and Jane are still with us today, and live within fifty miles of Indianapolis.

At the age of sixteen, Wanda married a well-to-do farmer. Wanda's marriage did not get off to a good start. Her husband bought her a new car and she came over with it to take Kat, Mil, and Hattie for a ride. They rode down a gravel road and ended up rolling over and totaling the car. When Uncle Al picked everyone up, he said, "You girls had to be going awfully fast." Hattie, puffing out each word, replied, "Oh, no, Uncle Al, she really wasn't. She only had her foot to the floor."

Wanda and Jane's mother, Susie Huddleston, was a good seamstress. She made dresses for Mil and Kat from feed sacks. They strutted around in the dresses like they were high fashion. Susie was a young widow with several children of her own, yet she always had time for Mil and Kat. One day while Uncle Ed was visiting, Susie stopped by, as country folk often do. He had one knee shining through his pants.

Susie told him, "I'll take the pants home and patch them for you." When she returned them, she had put a Christmas tree on the knee. He liked it so much that he looked down and, blushing, asked if she could do the other knee. Uncle Ed had to be the only man in the area running around with Christmas trees on his knees.

Uncle Al owned and operated a huckster truck and delivered Beck's Store At Your Door. He carried almost anything one needed for the kitchen. When he got to someone's house and they had no money, Uncle Al bartered. Sometimes he took milk in exchange for eggs or butter. If there was nothing to barter and they were very much in need, he gave them staples and let them run a tab. He carried block ice, which was a must for homes in those days, and he brought home a block of ice for our icebox when needed.

Kat was one of the first to help Uncle Al on his route. She loved it because it gave her a break from house chores. George, Ed, and Mil also helped on the huckster truck. Ed was a boy with a sharp tongue who often got mad at Uncle Al for one thing or another. One time he saw Uncle Al whipping Jim and spouted off his mouth, "If you don't quit whipping him I won't work on your stupid truck anymore!" When Mil got older she worked at Frosty Burkes drive-in as a carhop. She liked working there much more than working on the huckster truck.

George worked for an elderly widowed neighbor who had a greenhouse in her home. He made fifty cents a day working in the greenhouse. He saved his money while working for her and other neighbors on their farms. With this money, George ordered one hundred baby chicks from a farm catalog. By the time the chickens arrived, Uncle Al had built a chicken house for them. This was the beginning of our chicken and eggs. Vic, George, Jim, and Ed worked for a nearby farm family. They loved the escape during the summertime. The lady in charge always fixed them a big fried chicken dinner instead of paying them. They loved that and looked forward to their days of work.

One evening, after a long day of work, Jim, Vic, and George sat down for a nice country dinner of fried chicken with all the trimmings. There was one piece of chicken left on the plate and George and Jim both reached for it. Well, Jim got it first, but it happened to be a head. Utterly shocked, Jim laid it back on the plate and said, "I am really too full." George and Vic had a hard time trying to hide their grins. After a hard day's work on the farm they always came home with feet dragging. They all found a spot around the potbelly stove in hopes of relieving their aches and pains.

Every Saturday was bath day. It took about twenty gallons of water to fill the galvanized tub. After four baths, the water had to be changed. Of course, everyone wanted to be first so they wouldn't have to wash in dirty water. In the summertime, we took our baths outside under the tree. Every other day of the week, we just had sponge baths and ear checks.

Chapter 3

Sunday was Katherine's day for ironing. She had to heat the old flat irons on the cook stove and finish in time to attend the 1 p.m. church service. Each child had two outfits for the whole week. While Kat ironed, Mil got everyone else ready for church. Sunday mornings were disastrous with everyone bustling around getting ready for church.

When Easter came around it was fun for all. Aunt Mil boiled six-dozen eggs and dyed them by soaking them in raspberry or beet juice. Then she was like a kid herself. She always helped hide them for the big hunt.

The Eminence Pentecostal Church was a rather small church. When our truck stopped at the door and we unloaded, that pretty much made a small congregation. When we opened the door with our freshly starched and ironed dresses and shirts, they knew the Woods had arrived.

The church was a God-fearing, sin-hating, pew-jumping, foot-stomping, and hand-clapping church. That church was more fun than a barn dance. Sometimes the people got in a circle with the guitar players joining in, and they sang every song they ever knew from memory. My brothers say the best part of the service was when we had pitch-in dinners and everyone chowed down. We ate well on those Sundays. Vic remembers one day well, when we were in an all-day service of church, dinner, and singing. Someone came in and announced that World War II had ended. This sticks in his mind because it meant his dad would come home soon.

We had a good church friend named Dorothy who played the guitar, wrote her own songs, and sang them in church. My brothers still sing her unpublished songs today. There was a couple at church and the lady sang through her nose while her husband clapped his hands upside down with his elbows sticking out. All the boys went around the house singing like the couple and acting silly until Aunt Mil caught them and gave them one of her stern looks.

I don't remember any of us being really sick. When we had a cold, Aunt Mil made her famous magic syrup: steamed, sliced onions and honey. That was what we drank for colds. Other medications consisted of castor oil, milk of magnesia, Mercurochrome and iodine.

When we had an earache, Aunt Mil blew cigarette smoke in our ears. If we had a boil, she wrapped a piece of bacon on the boil to bring it to a head. I remember things like pinkeye and carbuncles, and there was always ringworm. I hated that because of the name. I now know it is only a fungus.

We used to sneak green apples off the tree and when Aunt Mil discovered us, she made us take a dose of castor oil. I still haven't figured out her logic for the castor oil. We never visited a dentist until after we left Cloverdale. Some of us had the measles and she put sheets over the windows to darken the room. We had to stay there until our measles were almost gone.

The old house still stands and there is a beautiful lake on the property, full of fish. That would have been good to have in the old days when we lived there. Close by there is a new two-story house with a deck overlooking the woods and the lake. In my memories as a child, the old place was so big. Now having seen it as an adult, I am amazed that fourteen children and two adults could have survived in that small house. I am filled with many happy memories as well as sad ones.

John was caught smoking by our neighbor, Mrs. Barnes. She told him that was not a good thing to do, and he answered that he liked it. She said, "Every time you want a cigarette, say 'Get thee behind me, Satan!' and repeat it three times. Your desire for the cigarettes will go away." The boys had fun with that saying around the house.

Uncle Al's '39 Ford pick-up

Uncle Al once bought four new tires for his old '39 Ford pickup truck. Before they were mounted, John and Arvine decided the tires would bring in some good money to buy some candy, and they sold the tires for a nickel each. When Uncle Al went to mount the tires and found them missing, he asked the boys where the tires were and they answered, "Oh, we sold those old tires for you." When sweat beads started to appear on Uncle Al's bald head, you knew you were in trouble. This day, it was popping out all over. Needless to say, they had to retrieve his tires from the buyer.

On one occasion we were all packed in the old truck like sardines. Uncle Al had made a camper shell from wood long before camper shells were even thought of. We were taking an exciting adventurous trip to Greencastle on a snowy, windy day. Uncle Al was driving along when suddenly he said, "Everyone hold on, we're going down!" It was the biggest hill I had ever seen. He guided it halfway down, then "Look out!" he called, and we flipped over a few times. Everyone crawled out of the windows one by one. Fear was running thick but the only injury was to Uncle Al's pride. We worked our way up the steep embankment and, after reaching the top which seemed endless, we all stood there trying to quiet down our breathing and collect our wits. Uncle Al flagged down help. It came--car after car loaded us all up and took us home. We had quite a caravan going back to the farm.

We lived together on the Cloverdale farm for four years before our lives changed again. Aunt Mil's nerves became very bad. She had a bad rash on her legs which hurt so badly that her legs would bleed. She also had headaches so severe that she often tied a bandana around her head and pulled it as tight as she could, in hopes of relieving the pain. Her doctor told her changes had to be made.

Aunt Mil and Uncle Al decided to sell the farm and move to Texas, where Uncle Al was born. That, of course, meant everyone could not go since we were a large part of her problem.

Back: Vic, Jim, and George
Middle (left): Arvine

Katherine was the only one to graduate from Cloverdale High School. The farm later sold for six hundred dollars at an auction. Farm life was a great experience, one I think every child could benefit from. We have a lot of pictures of the past, but we would not have them had it not been for Aunt Mil's love for family.

Aunt Mil, Uncle Al, and Arvine

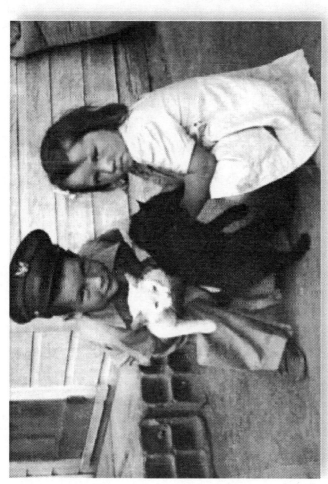

Leon and Norrie

Chapter 3

CHAPTER

4

Fun on the Farm

Isaiah 54:13

*And all thy children
shall be taught of the LORD;
and great shall be the peace
of thy children.*

Top: Ed and Jim
Middle: Mil
Bottom: Arvine, Aunt Mil, and Norie

Uncle Al and Aunt Mil both loved playing jokes on people. Uncle Al hooked up a rope with a bell on top for the front door. People were supposed to pull the rope to ring the bell when they came to the door. One time he positioned a bucket of water on top of the bell. When someone pulled the rope, the bucket of water dumped on his or her head. That was country fun in those days.

We had lots of fun with our outhouse. One time one of my uncles came home from the Army on leave. While there, he wired the outhouse seat for electricity and then added a switch in the house. When an unsuspecting victim sat down, my uncle would flip the switch and give them a nice big jolt. One time our neighbor Jane came flying out of the outhouse with her pants around her knees.

One day Aunt Mil sent Ed to get a bucket of water. When he returned with two buckets of water she threw one on him and said, "I said one." He stood there with his mouth hanging open, not knowing what to say. She had a gold tooth in the front of her mouth and she loved to show it off when she did things like that. Aunt Mil taught us all to smile. She loved to get Joan and me down and curl our hair on rags. I always loved it because it made such tight long curls, the kind of curl you love to wrap around your fingers.

One spring Uncle Al planted some new trees. He put old, used tires around them to protect them. One day he came home from work to find the tires were gone.

It seems George, Jim, and Vic thought they would be fun to roll down the lane in. Aunt Mil stood there trying to hide the smile that was creeping onto her face. Well, a real commotion broke out, he raised so much Cain. Each boy had to take the tires and put them back and swear they never would touch them again. "Since you have such an abundance of energy," said Uncle Al, "you can clean the chicken coop, too!"

Uncle Al loved hunting. Maybe it was just cheap food for the many mouths he had to feed. He often went out to get his limit of squirrels, rabbits, and an occasional pheasant. Sometimes the boys went with him, but I think he preferred going alone. It was probably the only peace and quiet he ever got. Every time he got a squirrel, he cut off its tail and tacked it to the side of the old shed. It was fun to see how many we ate each season. We always had plenty of fried squirrel and gravy.

I remember one time when we were all so excited because we were going to a bubblegum blowing contest in town. We already had our bubblegum in our mouths, getting it ready for the big contest. We were all packed in the old pickup truck and driving down the lane, when we ran into

Uncle Al's brother Ace and his wife who had come unexpectedly for a visit. We had to turn around and go back home and we never made it to the contest.

We were lucky to have enough money for food. There definitely was not enough money for basketballs or sports equipment, so the boys made basketballs by rolling up rolls of rope and securing it somehow into a ball. The basket for basketball was an old bottomless clothesbasket they hung up on a tree. With so many kids around, there was no problem finding a team. The old lane was used for many things. The boys got inside old tires and pushed each other down the lane. They still talk about that today. There were swings made out of grapevines.

On rare occasions Uncle Al pulled out his large battery-powered radio, usually at night. We gathered around, with the breeze flowing through the screens. Everyone settled down to their own comfortable spot and listened to the Grand Ole Opry on Saturday nights and heard Little Jimmy Dickens. Popcorn and hot chocolate were a rarity but fun at those times.

Aunt Mil was a big kid at heart and she loved getting in there and playing with us. She was a great storyteller. Ghost stories were fun at night while gathered around the potbellied stove and were made more exciting by the hooting of the night owls. Aunt Mil's mighty voice made the stories so real we surely believed them. Today our sister Mil loves to do the same thing to our kids when we have family wiener roasts.

There never was a shortage of entertainment on the farm. Aunt Mil gave each of the boys ten pennies and they did a penny toss against the house. The one who got closest to the house was the big winner. Those pennies could last a mighty long time.

One time the boys went skinny-dipping in a nearby pond. The owner came out hollering and they got so scared they ran home without their clothes. They had to go back and get them. Aunt Mil had a saying: *"If you have one boy you have a whole brain. If you have two boys, you have half a brain. If you have three boys, you have no brain at all!"*

Joan, Ed, and Paul used to go to our barn to play church. Paul, standing in the loft, was the preacher. Joan was seated at a bench and was the pianist. Sitting cross-legged on a bale of straw was Ed, the pew filler. Paul became quite animated, stomping his feet, waving his arms, and wagging his finger at Ed as he began preaching. "You must be born again or you will go to a burning hell!" Ed, repeating what he had seen in church, stood up and fell straight backwards pretending he was in the spirit. He

Paul

fell on a rusty nail and got blood poisoning in his leg. Aunt Mil said, "That's what you get for poking fun at church."

One day Arvine, Jim, and George decided to throw Trixie, the dog, in the neighbor's pond to see if she could swim. They got home and were laughing about it but Uncle Al didn't think it was so funny. The dog survived, but the boys were not sure if they would. They never tested Trixie's aquatic skills again.

Lightning bugs were always fun to catch. Aunt Mil saved jars for us to put the bugs in, and we counted them to see who caught the most. We tore off their lights and used them for rings. Today I wouldn't even touch one.

The boys made a tree house from scrap wood. If one of them wanted to escape chores, they hid in the tree house. When they were found out, their chores were increased.

One day some of the boys came home huffing and puffing, carrying a bundle of small black and white animals. They said, "Look! We have found a family of baby kittens." Soon they found out they were baby skunks. Needless to say, they were gone in a hurry!

The boys made homemade slingshots and placed tin cans on a fence to see who could hit the most cans.

Uncle Al made sleds. One was 5 feet by 7 feet to hold everyone. Of course, it was always fun pulling the sled back up the hills. After sledding we were ready for homemade ice cream that Aunt Mil made from snow. She was so good at making it that in the winter we prayed for snow.

Ed was the only one brave enough to sing this song to Aunt Mil: "*There's a place in France where the ladies wear no pants!*"

He continued to sing as Aunt Mil chased him around while he ran like a scalded dog.

Wednesday nights were happy times. In the summer, Main Street was closed and the Cloverdale grocery showed street movies. We took old blankets and spread out wherever we could, and Aunt Mil always popped a barrel of popcorn to take with us.

Sometimes we gathered in our living room and sang old songs like "Old Shep" and "Billy Boy", which Aunt Mil collected from the newspaper.

There are probably more good memories of the farm than bad ones. Our question today is, "Where would we have been without the help and love of Aunt Mil and Uncle Al?" They will be forever in our hearts. We know the things they did to discipline us were not abuse; they simply did not know how to handle that many children. Before going to the Children's Home we had settled into a real comfort zone at the farm.

Chapter 4

Clockwise from left:
George, Jim, Mil, Kat, Leon, and Norie

CHAPTER

5

Life in the Children's Home

Lamentations 5:3

*We are orphans and fatherless,
our mothers are as widows.*

Chapter 5

One day in 1947, we went for a drive. We were all loaded up in the pickup truck with the camper shell Uncle Al had made. Aunt Mil and Uncle Al took eleven of us to look at the Indiana Soldiers and Sailors Children's Home in Knightstown, Indiana. They meant well, but they could not stand the heartache of telling us what was about to happen to us. Aunt Mil, not knowing how to say goodbye, took us in and told us to look around, they would be back in a little while. They never returned.

We were taken to the administrative office where the admitting staff was expecting us. The next stop was the nurse's office for inspection. The head nurse stopped and put her hands on her hips, as if checking out all the sad faces. A hefty redhead, she looked like someone you wouldn't want to tangle with. Everyone checked out fairly well except Ed. From there we were separated into individual divisions. I think I sat on the step everyday for a week waiting for Aunt Mil and Uncle Al to return for us.

Of the six of us, four went to the children's home. Kat and Mil were old enough that they did not have to go. The painful thought of the trip was that we did not have a chance to say goodbye to Mil and Kat, who had no idea what was happening to their family until after the fact. We all came from a tough breed and we had built up a shield to keep us from feeling the pains of life.

Kat lived with our preacher's daughter while looking for a job. She found work at Indiana Bell Telephone Co. and eventually was able to afford her own efficiency apartment. She worked all week and every other weekend, but on her days off, she took the bus to the home to visit us for the weekend. Sometimes she brought a picnic lunch or small gifts.

Kat worked with a girl named Jean Brodie who introduced her to her brother Bill who was an airplane mechanic for the FAA. They started dating and later married. Bill loved to visit the kids at the home with Kat and enjoyed watching the boys play sports. Occasionally, Kat and Bill took the boys into town for dinner and special treats.

Mil went to Texas with Aunt Mil, Uncle Al, and Arvine. She worked in Houston for a while but returned to Indianapolis to work at the Standard Brand factory so she could spend time with us at the home. Mil always has been the mother figure to all of us.

When George, Jim, Leon and I, Norie, had to live at the home, it was really rough for Kat and Mil because it was the first time our family had been separated. Joan and Vic went to live with their father and stepmother where their lives began a roller coaster event. Our other cousins--Ed, John, Paul, Hattie, and Ella--stayed with us at the children's home as well.

Jim, Ella, Paul, and Leon

The children's home was spacious with expansive grounds, large buildings and factories, and a beautiful lake where we liked to ice-skate in winter. There was a bakery, dairy barn, print shop, woodworking shop, powerhouse, and a farm where the older children worked and learned trade skills.

Back: Jim and George
Front: Leon

There were individual divisions in each building, with twelve to thirty children per division. Each division had house parents, all very nice and caring people. There were planned activities in every division; some had Ping-Pong tables and challenging games of rummy, euchre and pinochle.

The girls' divisions were on one side of the lake and the boys' were on the other side. Ella and I were in Division #22 and Hattie was in Division #24 so the three of us got to see each other often. Each child made new friends in our new home, but it was far different from our crowded farm.

Every Sunday we were required to go to the chapel for church services. It was certainly nothing like the church we attended in Eminence. The chapel service was a cut-and-dry fight to stay awake, and we sang "Trust and Obey" every Sunday. To this day this is not one of my favorite hymns.

Ed had surgery on his neck shortly after we arrived at the children's home. The surgeons released the tendons in his neck that were causing him to hold his head to one side. He wore a neck cast for six weeks.

John had rheumatic fever twice while at the home and wasn't expected to live past the age of twelve, but he is still with us today.

Everyone adjusted fairly well to his or her new surroundings except for one person. That was me, the baby. I was only seven years old when I lost Aunt Mil, the only mother I had ever known. The only time I got to see my brothers was on Saturdays when we went to the candy store to buy candy with the tickets we got from the bank. I used to sit on the steps and wait for the milkman to bring the milk. The milkman was my brother George and he worked in the dairy.

Our father was still around when we went to the children's home. I remember I was on summer vacation with a sponsor from the home when our father died. They did not tell me until after I returned to the home so as not to ruin my vacation. Since I was only seven, I really didn't know him very well, and remember not being too upset about his death.

A lot can be said about our father. He had his strengths and many weaknesses. When I was five years old, someone inquired about adopting me from the family.

Chapter 5

He stood his ground and insisted that no matter what, his children would stay together.

At seventeen, Mil was living in Houston, and had a very vivid dream about Dad. She decided to look him up when she came up to Indianapolis. On her next trip she went to Kat's house and inquired about Dad. Kat sank down into the sofa and said nothing for a while, then with a tear running down her cheek, she quietly answered, "Mil, Dad is dead." That was the first Mil had heard about him. "He died yesterday," Kat told her. Since Mil had been traveling on the train, they could not tell her, so it was quite a shock when she heard the news.

It wasn't until years later that I learned the real story of his death. After our mother's death and while we were living in Cloverdale, my father met and married a woman he met in a tavern. She loved drinking and partying, so they drank and fought together. I now believe that, having lost his wife, family, and home, he had nothing to live for. He was weak, gave in to the bottle, and landed in jail several times due to his drinking. He was told if he came back one more time he would never see the outside again. As fate of the bottle would have it, he and the woman got into another fight and she stabbed him several times, resulting in seventy stitches. Sometime later, he got into trouble with her and ended up in jail again. The next morning they found him hanging in his cell. We still do not understand his doing this, if he did.

The home eventually contacted Aunt Mil and told her they found me crying every night at bed check. The staff at the home thought it would be better for me if she came and took me to Texas with her. I remember the lady coming in every night. She always found me crying, but I really don't know why I was crying. Aunt Mil came to Knightstown, and I went to Texas to live with her and Uncle Al.

I stayed in the children's home about a year and a half. A small glimmer of hope had ignited within me; however, I was too young to know I was leaving my whole family, only to face more sadness.

Cousin John decided after a while the home was not for him and he ran away a few times. Once he made it to Oklahoma before the police picked him up and returned him to the home. On his next attempt he made it all the way to Aunt Mil's house in Texas.

Chapter 5

She called the authorities and told them he could stay with her.

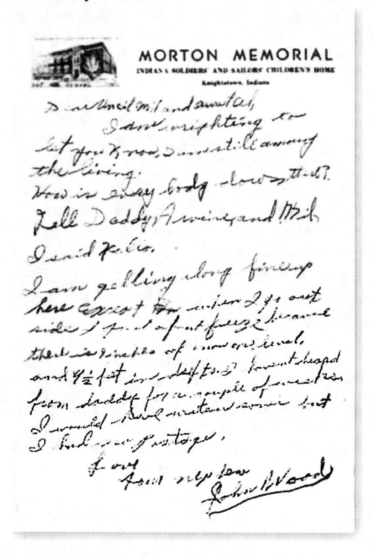

John's letter to Aunt Mil and Uncle Al

In the years that followed, Aunt Mil eventually got several more of us. I am sure that, to this day, the children's home never has taken on such an enormous task as the Wood crew!

In 1953, tragedy struck cousin Paul at the age of sixteen while in the children's home. He worked in the powerhouse and loved his work. He came home from school one day and said he did not feel well and wanted to lie down to take a nap. He never woke up; he died in his sleep. We still do not know the cause of his death. His parents didn't seem to care and no one ordered an autopsy.

After Paul's death, life was very hard for his brother Ed and his sisters Ella and Hattie, who were still in the home. Ed left the home and went to live with a family in Cloverdale. Soon he left Cloverdale and went to Aunt Mil's in Texas, and eventually joined the Army. Later, Hattie and Ella also left the home and joined Aunt Mil in Texas.

Ella and Paul were close in age and very close as brother and sister so she had a hard time dealing with his death. Ella was very talented and played the piano in the church we attended. It was fun having her back with me in Texas.

Leon, who was very shy and did not make friends easily, had a difficult time adjusting to the home also. I'm sure the treatment he received from Aunt Mil and Uncle Al was part of the cause of his problems. Leon stayed at the home until he was eighteen, and then went to Chicago with Mil, who by that time had married.

When he was unable to find a job, he decided to enlist in the Navy, but was there for only two years. It was peacetime and they were releasing some personnel early and he chose to leave the military. He went to Chicago and became a meat cutter. He has been a journeyman meat cutter all his adult life; now he is semi-retired.

Jim, who was older, adjusted well to the home environment and made friends very easily. He was a starter on the football team in high school and was a Ping-Pong tournament champion.

As most boys did, Jim and others in his division smoked. The boys took turns making cigarette runs to a small town three miles from the home, walking through the woods so no one would see them. One evening on the way back from a cigarette run, Jim ran into a skunk. The skunk was frightened and sprayed him. When he got back to the division, the housemother, twitching her nose, told him to go bury his clothes and take a bath. He slept on the porch that night. It was late spring so it was not too cold to sleep outside. The cigarettes were ruined and that was the last cigarette run he ever made.

In his senior year, Jim ran away a couple times. The first time the home took him back. The second time he was on his way to Indianapolis when two Legionnaires picked him up. They took him to a restaurant, fed him, and asked if he wanted to graduate from high school. He said yes so they explained to him that at his age if he ran away again, the home did not have to take him back. So he returned to the home and never ran away again. He was the only one of us to graduate from the children's home. After high school, Jim got a job in Indianapolis working at Inland Container. He worked there several months, then enlisted in the Army in 1955.

The irony of this saga is that Aunt Mil had to give us up for health reasons yet, one by one, some of us returned to our Aunt Mil and Uncle Al's home. They were really the only parents we ever knew. I often wonder if they took all of us in because they knew from experience what orphanages were like and wanted to save us from that torment.

When the eleven of us went to the children's home, Vic and Joan went to live with their father George and his new wife. Vic recalls when his father came home from WWII, he suffered from flashbacks. One time, when Vic was only twelve, his father imagined a battle with the enemy. They were riding with a friend in his truck one evening when suddenly George shouted, "Stop the tank! Stop the tank!" and he jumped out of the still-moving truck. Quickly the driver tossed a flashlight to Vic and told him to follow his dad.

Their adventure took them deep into the woods, sometimes crawling on their hands and knees and sometimes on their bellies. They even crossed a barbed wire fence. George constantly told Vic to turn off the flashlight so as not to be seen by the enemy. Even when George lit a cigarette, he cupped his hand around the match so the enemy could not see the small light. All night long they faced the enemies in George's mind until daybreak, when the flashback ended. Vic was not afraid during this episode since it had happened before and would happen many times again.

Later Vic and Joan went with their father to Oklahoma. Once there, George announced they would move to California; however, the move did not include the children.

Joan, at age 13, was sent back to Indianapolis on the bus to stay with her mother, Hazel; however, she had no earthly idea where to find her. She arrived in Indianapolis at 1:30 a.m. with $3 in her pocket. She went to the restroom thinking she would be safe until morning, but the cleaning lady reported her, thinking she was a runaway. The police came and took her to the police station. When they eventually found her mother, Joan lived with her for two years, until she was married. Hazel had little, if any, influence on Joan and Vic's lives.

Vic was left in Oklahoma to fend for himself at 15, and hopefully keep himself off the streets. In the warm months he had a job at a golf course as a caddy and made $2.50 for an 18-hole round. He also had a newspaper route in the mornings, evenings, and on weekends, with 180 customers during the week, and 300 on the weekends.

He won a contest for all his hard work and the prize was a trip to Galveston, Texas, but he was unable to go because he had no presentable clothes or shoes for the trip. When the school discovered he was living by himself, this meant there had to be changes. Vic moved in with his paper route manager for a while.

Finally he had to give up all his jobs and think about going back to Indianapolis. He sold his bike for $20, and since his bus ticket to Indianapolis was $17, he had $3 in his pocket when he arrived in the city, where he lived with his mother and stepfather until he married.

Joan   *Vic*

CHAPTER

6

Life In Texas

Psalms 72:12-13

For he shall deliver the needy when he crieth; the poor also, and him that hath no helper. He shall spare the poor and needy, and he shall save the souls of the needy.

Chapter 6

My life in Houston was different and challenging. For a while, it was just Aunt Mil, Uncle Al, cousin Arvine, and myself. Aunt Mil had developed a love for flowers and had a yard full of Crepe Myrtles. The house had a tin roof and wooden floors with the dirt showing through the floors. There were cockroaches and scorpions running around the house and scorpions stung me a few times. One of my chores was doing the dishes with cousin Arvine. Often we left out an open mayonnaise jar to see how many cockroaches we could catch. We caught a lot but it was never enough.

We attended church regularly--Sunday mornings plus Sunday, Wednesday, and Friday nights. That was about all we got done. I always liked the baptismal services. I was baptized in the San Jacinto River. That was a very meaningful and memorable experience.

Many times two young men in white shirts knocked on our door and wanted to convert us to the Mormon religion. One Saturday Aunt Mil asked them not to come back since we were secure in our own faith. The following Saturday, while Aunt Mil was napping, there was a knock at the door and it was the same pair of young men. When she saw them, she asked them to wait a moment. She returned with a broom and chased them all the way down the street. They were really doing some high-stepping and they never returned.

Across the street from us lived Irene, a dear friend from church. She was a stout, well-girdled lady who was crippled from birth and never had married. Two or three times a week she watched for my school bus to stop and flagged me down to come in for a visit. She always had a fried egg and pickle sandwich ready for me. Irene developed cancer and became very ill. She had a colostomy and Aunt Mil went over a couple times a day to take care of her. When Irene died it left a vacant spot in my heart for a long time.

Our rough life just followed us around. Money was in short supply in Texas, too. When Mil was there one time, the electric bill had not been paid and the man came to collect the amount due or cut off the electricity. Aunt Mil did not want to face him so she hid behind the door and told Mil where the money was. Mil answered the door and told him, "Wait just a minute. I know she left the money here someplace."

He waited, then she said, "I can't find the money." He answered, "Lady, that's it! I'm outta here. I can't wait any longer. I will have to turn your lights off." At that, Aunt Mil ran out from behind the door and gave the money to Mil. Mil hollered after the fellow, "I found it!" He said, "Well bless your heart, you're a little gold digger," and Mil replied, "Just call me Nancy Drew."

Aunt Mil applied for help from the Salvation Army. That meant she had to work in return for the help, which I now know is the way things should be. She and I went downtown and washed dishes in their big kitchen in return for their help. As an innocent child, unaware of the purpose of our trips, I thought it was great--the bus rides downtown, the huge kitchen, and more dishes than I had seen in my lifetime. It was fun to hear the clatter of all those dishes.

I remember we were invited to one Christmas party from the Salvation Army. They asked me to list things I wanted for Christmas. I put two things on the list--a boy doll and a set of jacks. When I was given my presents at the party, I took each piece of paper from the present, with my heart pounding very fast, and hoping for a boy doll. There he was with his overalls, plaid shirt, and eyes that opened and shut. Just what I had dreamed of, I gave him a name right there at the table--"Leon", after my brother. I still have Leon today. I always shall remember my one special Christmas party. I mastered the jacks very well and became good at putting the eggs in the basket and pigs in the pen.

We never celebrated Thanksgiving at Aunt Mil and Uncle Al's house, at least not that any of us remember. When Aunt Mil was much younger, her mother had died on a Thanksgiving Day, and we always wondered if that had something to do with their never getting excited about the holiday.

We had propane gas to heat the house. We took the hose and filled balloons with gas, tied notes on them, and then released them in the air. We wanted to see if someone would find the balloons, read the notes, and write to us in Houston. We never did get a reply.

While living in Houston, Uncle Al bought a full-size, life-like pony and bucking bronco on a stand. Off we went on the weekends to take pictures of people on the bronco and horse. When we returned home, we developed the pictures in the darkroom. I loved working with him and it was fun to see the pictures come to life right in front of our eyes.

Uncle Al bought a concertina accordion, and this was his toy. The accordion and its pretty sounds intrigued Ella and me. Even though it was off limits to us, Aunt Mil would get it out and let us play it while Uncle Al was at work. Ella was quite good and could play any instrument. The accordion seemed to talk when she and her dad, Uncle Ed, played it. They played music by ear but I had to work hard to learn to play the accordion. The first song I learned was "What a Friend We Have in Jesus". Uncle Al never learned to play since he really never had the time to put into it. When Uncle Al passed, Aunt Mil gave me the accordion, which I still cherish and love.

When Aunt Mil and Uncle Al first went to Houston, he drove a school bus, which suited him since he was so good with kids...he had plenty of practice. One evening he stopped by a grocery store to cash his paycheck and walked right in on a robbery. The thieves threw him and everyone else into the freezer. He always remembered that cold experience!

Later Uncle Al was a night watchman for a pipeline company in Houston. While working there he met a young man by the name of Chester Chase. Chet was a good-looking man and a hard worker with naturally curly hair and pretty, white teeth. One night Uncle Al forgot to bring his watchdog, Scotty. Arvine, who also was at work there, offered to go home for the dog. He invited Chet to go along so he could introduce him to his cousin Mil. They searched every room but couldn't find the dog. Just as they were leaving, a beautiful brunette showed up on the porch--Mil. It must have been love at first sight because Uncle Al never got his dog that night.

In 1949, when I was ten years old, Mil and Chet were married in a small country church. I remember sitting in the front row crying the whole time, knowing they would be leaving me.

They made frequent trips back and forth to see all of us. One time Chet visited me on a run to Houston. Aunt Mil and I had been discussing a school May Day dance. I needed material for a special dress, but Aunt Mil said there was no money for material, so I would not be able to go to the dance. Chet overheard our conversation and when he was leaving, he took my hand and placed a folded ten-dollar bill in it. I was so excited, I said, "Oh my gosh! Is it real?" and everyone laughed at that. I bought the material, had the dress made, and went to the dance. I'll always remember that.

Mil and Chet lived in Monroe City, Louisiana, and they sent me bus tickets to visit them during the summer. Aunt Mil said I could stay three weeks, but we called to ask if I could stay a couple more weeks. Usually she said yes. Mil and I ate a lot of butterscotch sundaes, which was a treat for me. I do believe we lived on them.

When Mil and Chet were traveling on the pipeline, I rode with Mil in the car for a while and then with Chet in the truck. I didn't last long riding with him because he concentrated on driving and didn't talk much. Consequently, I had him stop and let me ride with Mil. We made many unauthorized stops for all my transfers.

Mil was pregnant with her first child when Chet was drafted into the Army in 1953. Little Steve was born a few months before Chet returned from the Korean War. When he came back, they moved to Chicago so he could go to school on the GI Bill. He attended Lincoln Technical Institute, a diesel mechanic's school, and after completing that program, he took a course in heating and air conditioning.

One summer Mil sent me a train ticket for a vacation in Chicago, and Aunt Mil said I could stay three weeks. At one of the train station stops, while I was sitting at a table eating, a man came up to me and said, "Our table is over here." Apparently, he had gone to the restroom and lost the girl he was with. She walked up while he was standing there, and a look of shock shot over all our faces because she looked exactly like me! That poor red-faced man didn't know which one to take.

Mil and I had a wonderful three weeks and time passed much too fast. We pushed Steve around in the awkward, antique buggy like we owned the streets. Toward the end of my visit, Mil became very ill and since Chet was at work, I called an ambulance. When they took her away, two-year-old Steve and I hung out the second floor apartment window crying. It turned out Mil had a miscarriage, so I called for permission to extend my visit and got another two weeks. Mil and I always had tried to figure a way to get more time to spend together; however, we never expected it to happen this way.

Mil and Chet also sent for Jim and Leon to visit during the summer vacations. Once, on the train trip back to the home, Jim wrote a letter to them saying he was having a hard time with Leon and that he cried the whole way back. He mentioned what a great time the two of them had and how much they missed Mil and Chet already. I ran across this letter a short time ago, and it still brings a lump to my throat today. The summer vacations were great for the boys, but the vacations made it all the more difficult to return to the orphanage.

When I was about eleven years old, Uncle Ed, Ella's father, came to Houston and lived with us for many years. Every day when we left for school, he said to Ella and me, "Girls, watch out for those cars. They are bigger than you are. You can't hurt them, but they can hurt you." I remember we always laughed after hearing the same thing for so long. He was as tough as scrap metal, but he was very good to us.

When I was twelve, Aunt Mil and I visited Greencastle, Indiana, where Kat and George shared an apartment. Mil joined us there. Mil was fixing my hair and I asked why everyone called our aunt, Aunt Mil, while I called her Mother. Mil explained to me that our mother died when I was very young. Aunt Mil came into the room and overheard our conversation. She slapped me and told Mil she had no right to tell me about our mother. A storm of emotions and anger filled the air. My heart was beating like a typewriter gone wild. We left immediately for Indianapolis. For me it was an emotional separation. When we left I was crying and Mil carefully wiped away the unwanted tears and said, "Everything will be okay."

I attended Smiley Junior High School in Houston, and I sang in the choir. It was so much fun to travel to other schools and perform for them. Aunt Mil was very protective and strict about where I could and could not go. For example, I was not allowed to go bowling or to movies--that was too worldly--but I was allowed to attend the outdoor roller skating rinks.

After completing the eleventh grade, I dropped out of school to get a job. I found one in downtown Houston as an elevator operator. It was a fun and interesting job. That was in the days when 10-15 people got on the elevator at once, and everyone called out a different floor. Then they got mad when you didn't remember to stop on their floor. That job definitely had its ups and downs. A 50- to 60-hour workweek was not uncommon. My checks were divided three ways. First, I paid for my keep at home. Next I paid tithes to the Lord. The rest went into the bank for the future.

Arvine met a girl named Yvonne at a church picnic and they married very young. He was seventeen and she was just sixteen, and they lived with us for a while. Aunt Mil backhanded me for the slightest thing, and this bothered Yvonne. She told Arvine she could not stay there and watch that kind of treatment of a child. He told his mother and it must have had an effect because after that she did not hit me when they were there. I loved that security.

It wasn't long before they started having children. Oh, how I loved those babies. I played with them and enjoyed having them there. Yvonne worked while they lived with us. She took turns with Ella and me: one week she spent her check on clothes for Ella, then the next week she spent the check on me. This didn't happen all the time, just on special occasions. We thought it was because we helped with the children while she worked. When they moved to the country, I loved to visit them.

Arvine always smoked small cigars and I thought they smelled really good. One time he said, "Here, you want to smoke one?" and I eagerly accepted. "Puff it," he said. So I puffed. "Again," he chuckled. So I put the cigar into my mouth and drew in a deep breath as if it were my last. When I started coughing on the smoke, I thought it *was* my last breath! "I think I don't like smoking," I said sheepishly, going to the army cot to lie down as the whole room started spinning. By this time he was laughing like a wild man. That was the first and last time I ever tried smoking. Many years passed and whenever I saw Arvine, he would laugh and ask, "You want a cigar?"

I recall coming home from school one day and Aunt Mil met me at the door. She was complaining about my dirty closet and told me to go immediately in there and clean it up. When I opened the closet door there stood my brother George, home on furlough from the Army. I was so excited to see him. We had a great time while he was home. He took me shopping and bought me two new dresses. I was so happy to have new clothes to wear.

I still missed my brothers and sisters and I kept in touch by writing letters. I had to be careful what I wrote because Aunt Mil insisted on reading all of my outgoing and incoming mail. If I had something to write that I didn't want her to see, I would slip the letter to Yvonne to mail for me, and tell the person that I wrote not to mention the letter in the return mail. When my brother Jim wrote to me, he always signed his letters and cards with the same ending, "Your Loving Brother, James Wood".

Mil divided her time between Texas and Indianapolis so she could visit with both the boys at Knightstown and with me in Texas. I looked forward to her coming to be with me in Texas; she was my big sister and I loved her dearly. We had so much fun when she was there. She worked at a fruit stand in downtown Houston and brought me maple nut goodies from work each evening. Things like that we never forget. We slept together on the rollaway bed in the kitchen. Mil sang songs to me and we played, laughed, and giggled like best friends do.

Mil and Chet came to Houston when I was eighteen. I decided I wanted to live with them in Chicago, but I was afraid to tell Aunt Mil. With a hundred questions knocking at my brain, I knew this is what I wanted to do, but it would be difficult. Mil and I packed my clothes in paper bags while in my bedroom. Several times when we heard Aunt Mil coming down the hall, we tossed the bags in the closet. When we finally were packed and ready to go, I swallowed hard and told Aunt Mil I would like to go to Chicago for a visit. She threw the worst fit I had ever seen her throw. She knew I was going to stay with Mil. It hurt her very much but it was a decision that had to be made. I now know it was the best decision for my life.

Aunt Mil and Uncle Al

CHAPTER

7

Life in Chicago

Psalms 68:6

God setteth the solitary in families:
Beloved, let us love one another:
For love is of God.

Life in Chicago was so different from Houston, but it certainly was a magnificent adventure. Mil and I often went roller skating and we learned waltz dancing at the rink which was a lot of fun. I attended my very first movie with Mil at age eighteen. There was so much to see in Chicago; the museums were amazing plus they were free. Mil and I pushed her baby Steve in the old buggy and spent free time in the parks and on the lakefront. It was fun going to Lincoln Park Zoo, which was not

Donna, Norie, and Steve

only by the lakefront but also free. Mil had her second child about a year after I arrived.

When Jim and Leon came home from the service, they, too, went to Chicago and lived with Mil and Chet until they found jobs and could afford their own apartments. Leon was still very shy and he had a hard time keeping a job, so he was with us a little longer than Jim. It was great spending time with my brothers again. Ella also left Texas for Chicago, and lived with us for a short time. After we all were in Chicago, the Chases had to move to a larger apartment to accommodate all of us.

We lived in a basement apartment and my bed was under the window. One night after we all went to bed, a man crawling in the window awakened me. I lay there watching him, wondering if I should pretend to be sleeping. Suddenly he stepped on my leg and I shot out of the bed like a cannonball and jumped in the middle of Mil and Chet's bed. I was screaming, "Someone came in my window and stepped on my leg!" Chet ran into the kitchen where he found Jim standing. Jim said to Chet, "Norie scared me with her screaming more than I scared her." He had forgotten his door key and did not want to wake us up.

Needless to say, he had everyone up, even the people in the upstairs apartment.

One afternoon, Chet was working in the garage in the back of the apartment and Mil was lying on her stomach in the backyard trying to get a tan. All at once she felt someone tickling her legs. She said, "Chet, stop that!" When the tickling continued, she looked up. To her surprise, it wasn't Chet, but a rat! She jumped up onto the fence, screaming, and Chet came running to see what the problem was. He got Mil off the fence and after she told him what happened, he told her the rat was just looking for a warm place to stay!

My first job in Chicago was with Bankers White Cross Insurance. Mil and Chet would not let me pay rent so I could take care of my eyes and teeth. My eyes were very weak and I wore thick glasses. My first paycheck paid for contacts. I never visited a dentist until I was in Chicago.

After Chet finished his schooling, we returned to Indianapolis, our birthplace. Before going to Indianapolis, Mil and I made a trip to Houston to see Aunt Mil. One day she asked that we take her to the hardware store. We sat in the car with the doors locked, talking. After sometime, an old man came out and tried to open my door. Finding it locked, he went to Mil's door but it, too, was locked. Mil jumped out of the car and gave that poor man what for. She said, "You crazy thing! What do you think you are doing?" He looked amazed and visibly shaken, but said nothing and went back into the store. Soon Aunt Mil came out and asked, "Girls, what did you do? That was my feed man; he was bringing my chicken feed out to the car." We almost died. Even though we were grown, we had to do what we were taught as children--tuck tail and go in red-faced to apologize. We never took her to that store again.

Back: Betty, Phyllis, Bob, Chet
Front: Leon, George, Norie, Jim, Bev, Mil, Kat

CHAPTER

8

Death of the Becks

Psalms 23:2

He maketh me to lie down in green pastures: He leadeth me beside the still waters.

I returned to Houston to visit Aunt Mil and Uncle Al several times during the time I lived in Chicago. They never left my heart. Uncle Al was a good-hearted man even though I am sure there was resentment for having taken on all of the Wood crew. He was a hard worker all his life and he had a great influence on our lives.

Arvine and his wife came to Indianapolis for a vacation. While they were here, we had planned a big reunion with all the gang. When they arrived from Texas, they brought Aunt Mil with them to surprise all of us. She had cut her hair and they got her a permanent. She was having the time of her life and seldom was without her childish grin. Aunt Mil pulled out a small, galvanized bucket, and with a belt hanging from her neck, she started after the boys to get her water. Aunt Mil's softness began to emerge as she grew older.

On one of our trips to Houston, Kat, Mil, Arvine, and I went to the hospital to see his mother. Arvine was quite a prankster. We got on the elevator to go to the eleventh floor, at least that is what we intended to do. Arvine got on and did something he shouldn't have done and the elevator stopped between floors; we were stuck for twenty minutes. Kat, rubbing her hands and shuffling, said, "Arvine, you crazy thing. I promise you one thing if I live through this: I will never get on another elevator with you." After what seemed an hour, the door opened and there stood several doctors, nurses with orange juice, and three mechanics wondering what was wrong with their elevator.

Uncle Al died in 1967, after a long illness. Ten years later, several of us made a trip to Houston to try to improve Aunt Mil's quality of life. There was Mil, her daughter Angie, Kat, me, and my two girls Vonda and Londa. Mil and I had lived in Texas and knew what we were getting into. Kat had no earthly idea what an exciting week she was about to have.

The minute we entered the house, Londa said, "Oh, my goodness, what a big ant!" It was climbing up the wall and she proceeded to flatten it with her fist. It was not an ant but a huge flying Texas cockroach. That was it for Katherine. She said, "You crazy girls, you got me into this mess. I'm calling my daddy [her husband] to come and get me." We laughed so hard at her all week our sides ached. Kat didn't seem to join us in our laughter. Our girls never had seen anything like that place. They danced back and forth all week long so no bugs could land on them. They danced when they combed their hair or brushed their teeth. They spent time sitting in the middle of the bed playing cards and games. This was the only safe place from the bugs.

Our first cleaning project was the bathroom. Aunt Mil loved taking hot bubble baths but had allowed someone to fill her bathtub with old clothes. We filled five plastic garbage bags with the clothes and then promptly tossed them into the backyard. It took a whole bottle of bleach to clean the bathroom. Then we took Aunt Mil and put her into the tub for a special bubble bath treat. Oh, how she loved that, but she was still worried about the clothes we threw in the backyard. Later I got brave and decided to take a bath myself. My daughter Vonda came in and said, "Oh my gosh, Mom, there is someone sharing your water!" I looked around and there was a Texas cockroach floating in the water behind me. I almost made a new door in the bathroom. That was the end of my bath time while there--I went dirty.

After Kat decided she was not leaving, she began to work on fighting cockroaches. When she moved the kitchen table, the roaches dropped from the bottom of the table. She took jar lids and filled them with crushed roach tablets and placed them under each table leg. Mil and I moved from the bathroom into the kitchen to clean. While cleaning the cabinets, we threw out a box of old baseball cards. We did not know how valuable they probably were and frankly, we were too hot to care. We were in the Texas heat with no air-conditioning.

We pulled out the stove to clean behind it and found a dead rat. Aunt Mil had put out rat poison before we got there. The refrigerator gasket was worn out and the roaches were using it for a playhouse. We pitched the refrigerator and the stove into the backyard. The next day we passed the hat among relatives and bought her a new refrigerator and stove. By the time we left there, we did not see any pests during the daytime. Katherine did her job well.

Aunt Mil was afraid in her house and neighborhood. She slept all day and stayed up all night in her bedroom. She slid knives in the door facing, feeling more secure that way. While we were there, all of us slept in a cramped bedroom across from Aunt Mil. The room had a broken window covered with plastic. There was one bed and a cot, which I slept on. One night everyone was settled down, half asleep, when Angie dropped her arm in the pit of my stomach. I jumped out of that bed screaming, thinking someone, or something, had me.

Mil took a handgun along for protection and hid it under her pillow. Katherine asked, "What would you do if you saw an arm coming through the window?" Mil responded, "I would shoot that sucker off." Kat said, "Look, Mildred, if you start shooting, let me know. I don't want my head blown off."

We had a miserable week but made the best of a tough situation. We wanted to make Aunt Mil more comfortable in her later years. It was our turn to take care of her. Toward the end of the week, Aunt Mil came out of the bedroom shouting, "Girls! Girls! Elvis Presley just died!" She was a huge Elvis fan. We all ran into her room and watched the news report of his death.

Shortly before Aunt Mil had her stroke, Mil and I made another trip to Houston. Aunt Mil was in the hospital. When we arrived our first stop was to see her neighbor and dear friend, Ella Mae, a lovely black lady, who insisted we stay for dinner. She said, "Granny would never forgive me if I didn't feed you." We sat down in this lovely clean home to the most wonderful pork roast dinner we had ever had.

The next day we went to the hospital to see Aunt Mil and discovered her hair bushy, knotted, and in great need of care. Knowing that Ella Mae was a beautician, we called her and asked for help. She came up and we got permission to cut Aunt Mil's hair in the bed since she was too sick to sit up. She looked up and said, "Thank you, daughters," and that meant Ella Mae, too.

Aunt Mil died in 1980. She had a stroke that left her unable to see or speak very clearly. Mil and I visited her a week before she died. Knowing we never would see her again, we were crying as we left. Although it was hard to understand her, Aunt Mil comforted us, saying, "Girls, don't cry and worry about me because I will be safe in the arms of Jesus." She died one week later with a smile on her face, literally. The funeral director said he never had seen this before. She died knowing many loved her.

Aunt Mil and Uncle Al's only child, Arvine, was an over-the-road semi driver, carrying flammable materials. Thirteen months after his mother's death, he was killed while driving the semi. He lost control of the truck and it turned over and burned. Another motorist pulled him out of the truck but he died at the scene. How strange that he would die so soon after his mother. Arvine's wife of thirty years and his children--two daughters, Pamala and Deborah, and a son, Frankie--still live in the Houston area.

Back: Arvine, Aunt Mil, and Yvonne
Front: Deborah, Pamala, and Frankie

Arvine Beck

Chapter 8

Gone But Not Forgotten

Arvine Franklin Beck, age of forty-seven,
Has gone to be with God in Golden Heaven.
We will miss you, yes we will
Your boots on Earth we can never fill.

Gone onto Heaven leaving your wife
Down here with each other you had a good life.
Together you both shared the 30th year,
The love you showed was all so clear.

Your wife and family was your pride,
Your Special Love was hard to hide.
Two daughters and only one son,
Can't name the many things for us you've done.

You were the kindest man there will ever be,
Anyone who ever met you could always see.
All so wonderful, this you was,
Known to so many as "County Cuz".

Driving a truck you seemed to like,
Trucking on down talking in the mic.

Death of the Becks

A truck driver you was one of a kind,
Also known to others as "One Track Mind".

Out of the truck we wish you had gotten.
On your headstone we say "Gone but not forgotten".
What we say is OH so true,
Our lives without you will be so blue.

There will never be another man like you
Whose love for people was so true.
You brightened our lives so very bright,
You've left us, Daddy, but you are still in sight.

Someday we will all be with you again,
We'll have to go on living without you until then.
But until we meet at those Pearly Gates,
THANK YOU, DADDY, FOR BEING SO
GREAT.

I LOVE YOU AND WILL MISS YOU
DEARLY.
YOUR DAUGHTER,
PAMALA

Chapter 8

CHAPTER

9

Life in Indianapolis

Psalms 71:23

My lips shall greatly rejoice
when I sing unto thee;
and My soul, which thou hast rescued.

- ## My Sister Katherine

Kat and Bill always have lived in Indianapolis, and they have three children, Greg, Jeff, and Marsha. Bill worked for Link Belt on the west side of Indianapolis. He had a major stroke that left him paralyzed on one side and unable to speak. For eight years Kat was his constant companion, wife, and caregiver until he died of lung cancer in 1996.

Greg is a geologist for the Tennessee Valley Authority and teaches geology at the University of Tennessee. He has three children. Jeff is a schoolteacher. He and his wife, a nurse, have been missionaries to Africa for three years, and they have two daughters. Marsha is married with two children and works for a mortgage company.

- ## My Sister Mildred

Mil is still our mother figure and always is there for all of us. After a few years working for Schilling Chilling Heating and Air Conditioning, Chet started his own company specializing in commercial heating and air-conditioning. He is still working today.

Mil and Chet have three children. Steve has been working in the family business since 1970. After five years, he became a journeyman. Now he is married with five children. Donna, who works as a manager for Lancôme Cosmetics, is married and has three children. Angie, an RN for an Indianapolis hospital, is married and has two children.

Mil stays busy with all of them, and she never ceases to amaze us with her tireless energy. Mil and Kat's children all are very close in age and have become best friends.

She and Chet have been married for fifty-four years and are now in their seventies. Mil, the strongest heart of all, has found that even her powerful heart has its limits--she was diagnosed with cardiomyopathy many years ago.

▪ My Brother George

George came to Indianapolis when he returned from the Korean War. He worked downtown and everyday he had lunch at the five and dime, where he met his future wife, Phyllis. She won and they have been married for forty-seven years.

They have two children, Debbie and Gary. When the children were young, George moved his family to Cloverdale. They had a small house on the main highway in town. Debbie and Gary both graduated from Cloverdale School. Both are married with children now and live in Indianapolis.

George was very pale and weak as a child, but now he is the life of our family outings. He plays basketball and volleyball with all of the nieces and nephews and usually beats them. All the children want George to play on their team.

George and one of his friends from the children's home in Knightstown always attend Legion Day and Homecoming each year. There they play basketball with the children who are in the home now. George says he and his friend are the only seventy-year-old spry men on the court.

While he was in the Army, George met and became good friends with a fellow by the name of P. F. Parker. This is the story of their reunion many years later, as it appeared in the local Philadelphia, Mississippi, newspaper.

42-year Search Finally Reunites Army Buddies

George and P. F. Parker

Forty-two years of searching ended this week for a couple of war buddies catching up on lost time. P. F. Parker's dream since coming home from the Korean War has been to find his comrade in arms, George E. Wood, just to thank him one more time. His wife said that he remembered George well and it was his life-long dream to find George and talk to him before he died.

Parker, 69, of Philadelphia, Mississippi, suffers from diabetes and rheumatoid arthritis. He has been sick for the past twenty years and hasn't walked in nine.

Parker and Wood, who lives in Indianapolis, were Army cooks together in Korea. "I remember him well," Wood said. "We used to play pitch and catch, sang hymns, played ping pong, cards--whatever we could do to kill time."

113

The reason they were so close was that they didn't drink, cuss, or smoke. That is why they always hung around together-- because they were so much alike.

Parker was wounded and sent home three months earlier than Wood, and the two lost contact. They never stopped remembering their times together.

"Parker wrote out a copy of the song "The Old Country Church" when we were in the service, I still have it. When I get it out to sing I always think about him." When Parker recuperated from his war wounds, the search for Wood began. Parker and his family, determined to find Wood, went through all the steps to locate someone-- searching telephone directories, placing ads in newspapers and magazines, and using the Internet.

The Parkers put it in a thing called Finders, Seekers. They sent in $15.00 and they sent back 800 names. When The Parkers realized none of the names listed were the right man, they still kept trying. Finally Parker's son, Tim Parker, called the Veterans Affairs Hospital in Indianapolis, where Wood was from, and put the search to an end. "He talked to a social worker but she wasn't allowed to tell us where we was.

She said she would tell Wood that we were looking for him, but Wood would have to do the calling. He called us back that day and we talked for forty minutes." After finding each other, the two talked about the possibility of meeting again in person. Wood's niece worked as a flight attendant at an airline and she offered George a flight pass to visit Parker. Wood flew to Jackson, and Parker met him at the airport. "We were real proud to meet after all this time. It was great to see Wood again," Parker said. "I just can't explain it."

P. F. Parker and George

Parker passed away one year after their reunion.

■ **My Brother Jim**

In 1961, Jim left Chicago and went to Indianapolis and worked as a journeyman meat cutter. He worked for the same grocery that Leon worked for at the time.

Jim met his wife, Beverly, in 1962 and they were married in 1963. Bev had been married before and had three children, Rick, Leigh Ann, and Marshall. The children were young and they loved Jim and considered him their dad. Jim rose to the challenge and did quite well. Rick, the oldest, has his own business in heating and air-conditioning. Leigh Ann lives in Atlanta with her husband and two children, and Marshall is a brick mason.

Together Jim and Bev had two daughters. Cheryl, married with two children, lives in Las Vegas, and is an RN working in labor and delivery. Janet is a flight attendant and lives in Indianapolis.

Jim's hobbies were playing the guitar and singing. I remember when my husband's mother heard Jim sing for the first time, she said to him, "Honey, with a voice like that, you should be singing for the Lord." He did have a beautiful voice.

Jim also loved to fish. He and Bev traveled a lot and each summer they went to

Canada for part of their vacation so Jim could get his fill of fishing.

He went to work at Ford Motor Company in 1964, and retired from there in 1996, after 32 years.

When Jim developed non-Hodgkin's lymphoma of the brain, his prognosis was not good. The doctors said he had only a short time to live (six to twelve weeks.) His oncologist gave him experimental chemo and radiation therapy, and he was in remission for over six years. On one of his many trips to the hospital, a nurse asked him what were his favorite things to do, and he said loving his daughters, fishing, and singing. On a trip to Nashville, Jim recorded some songs at a recording studio.

Jim

His cancer returned in December 2001, and he became so ill that he had to go to a nursing home. All the brothers, sisters, and cousins rallied around him, taking turns in shifts caring for him and offering support.

However, he lost his battle for life in August 2002. At the memorial service for Jim, Bev played two songs he had recorded, "One Day at a Time" and "Why Me, Lord." He would have been proud knowing he was singing for his family and friends again. Jim's death has been very hard for all of us and we miss him daily.

- **My Brother Leon**

Leon came to Indianapolis with us when we left Chicago. He was still shy, but he had learned the meat-cutting trade in Chicago, and he found a job in Indianapolis at a large grocery chain. He met his wife, Betty, in 1964, and they have been married for thirty-five years. They have no children. Leon is semi-retired and still working as a meat cutter.

- **Norie (that's me!)**

I rented my very first apartment and worked for a large hardware chain in Indianapolis. It was fun having my own place. I made many friends at work and we went to parties, movies, and bowling, and in the summer spent time at the parks.

In 1962, a few years after I returned to Indianapolis, I met my future husband, Bob Crane, and it was love at first sight for me. We dated for over a year and married after he finished a six-month tour of duty with the Army.

We rented a cute house on the east side of Indianapolis. Soon after, I had my first child, Vonda. Thanks to my husband, I was able to be a stay-at-home mom. Three years later, we had our second daughter, Londa. We then bought our home in a suburb of Indianapolis, where we still live.

When Londa was born we were as excited as any parents can be, but we soon realized she was born mentally challenged. Some people call that a handicapped child but Londa is anything but handicapped. I call it mentally slow. With children like this, their handicap is usually other people's attitudes toward them. We once had a neighbor who said, "You should be glad Londa is not a Mongoloid idiot." Well, it didn't take me long to know who the real idiot was.

Londa can and does accomplish anything she attempts. She can keep up with any angler at his catch and she and Ed love to go fishing together. She has played the piano for many years. Mil's daughter, Donna, used to live on a lake and Londa wanted to water-ski so badly. After many failed attempts by herself, Vonda got into the water with her and helped her get the skis on and showed her how to hold them up when the boat started moving. Londa finally got up and thought she was the queen of the lake. We all cheered and screamed for her while Vonda was left behind in the water.

Londa keeps busy with bowling, swimming, and other sporting activities. She is active in the love that surrounds her. If the world had as much love and compassion for others as Londa has in her heart, the world would be a better place.

Bob, always a sportsman, loves to fish and hunt, and one of his goals was to open a sporting goods and gun shop. We opened a shop in Indianapolis and kept it for eight years. I ran the sporting goods shop during the week with the help of a couple employees. Bob ran the shop on the weekend when he wasn't working at the asphalt plant where he worked for twenty-four years until retiring in 2002.

When my daughter Vonda was fourteen in 1979, she became very ill. She had progressively worse headaches for a year and a half. She lost a lot of weight and her coordination was very bad. She had trouble swallowing, her speech was slurred, and her eyes jumped from side to side. To top it off, she had severe hiccups all the time. We had very good doctors but they could not figure out the problem.

Vonda was hospitalized many times for tests. One morning I was home spending time with Londa when the neurologist stopped by Vonda's hospital room. He told her, "If you think you've got pain, I will take you downstairs and show you some people that are really sick." Vonda did not really understand what he meant and called me to tell me what he said. He told her he would take her to the diabetic floor to see the patients with amputations. Another doctor called late one evening and told us that she only had three months to live. That helped me make the decision to go to Mayo Clinic in Rochester, Minnesota.

I made a fast telephone call to my sisters to see if they could go with us. We were all up all night packing and getting ready for the trip. Mil and her daughter Angie, Kat, and the three of us were going to make the trip.

Chapter 9

The next day we all got loaded up in my car with the fold-down camper attached. Well, we were so loaded down that we were touching the ground. Our neighbor's son, Mike, was just a kid himself. He was Vonda's age, fifteen, and they were good friends. He unhooked the camper and I was off to the automobile repair shop to get heavy-duty shocks installed. When we got back, Mike was waiting to hook us up again. As we left, poor Mike waved until we were out of sight. He probably was thinking, "They will never make it."

Off we went with the camper, but there was one problem. We had never pulled a trailer before and we could only go forward. We made the thirteen-hour drive with Vonda lying down most of the way.

While I drove everyone slept. I noticed the top of the camper had come loose and was flying up. I said, "Is it my imagination or has the top come loose?" Everyone woke up telling me just how to get off the road. We stopped and discovered the clip that holds down the corner had fallen out.

We were in the middle of nowhere and we didn't have a clue what we would do. Mil looked down at her feet and exclaimed,

"Look here!" It was a spike nail. We put it in where the clip should have been and we were off again in less than a minute.

When we arrived at the campgrounds in Rochester to park the camper, the attendant said, "Just park over between those two trees." We told him, "Well, we have never backed up a camper before." He threw his hands in the air and said, "Oh mercy, let me do it!"

We had gone to Mayo without an appointment, which is not a good idea. The camp manager told us to go straight to the hospital and he would take care of the camper. When we returned to the campground he had the camper set up with the lights on waiting for us.

We showed up at Saint Mary's hospital on a Sunday night. The next morning we had an appointment at the clinic, and by Friday we had an appointment with the Chief of Neurology and the Chief of Neurosurgery.

We went to the clinic for one week while staying in the camper. Everyone got the flu except one person. Who? Vonda! We all took turns heaving (and more!) outside the camper. The doctors decided Vonda required brain surgery, and although they did not know the problem, they intended to find out; however, they believed it was a brain tumor somewhere, perhaps in the brain stem or maybe outside the brain.

Before the surgery the girls all went home. Before leaving, Mil overheard an elderly lady saying she had $10 rooms for rent across the street from the hospital. Mil went over to her and said, "Excuse me, did I hear you say you have rooms for rent?" The woman answered so loudly, I jumped when she spoke, saying, "That is right, my lady. You have the right person." She took us to see her place and we had a beautiful small apartment for ten dollars a night. I only had to go out the back door and cross the street to reach the hospital. We were glad my sister had big ears and used them at the right time.

When my sisters got home, Bob left to come up for the surgery and drove all night in time to make it. The next day when they came to get Vonda for surgery, we were very worried and had no idea what to expect. The doctor said, "Don't worry, we will take good care of her." I told him I would be praying for him as well.

Halfway through the surgery, they came out and said it was not a tumor and

124

that she would be just fine. They found that the problem was Arnold Cheori Syndrome, a malformation at the base of the skull, and actually it is a mild form of Spina Bifida. The doctor came into her room and told her this problem usually doesn't show up until later in life. Vonda whispered, "I am unusual," and he patted her arm and said, "No, you are special."

While she was in Intensive Care, Vonda whispered to me, "Mom, I can see better already." I knew right away it was worth the trip. When we left the Mayo Clinic, one of her doctors said to her, "Vonda, when you came in here, did you have any idea we were so worried about you?" She shook her head and he said, "Well, when we see someone come in with hiccups around the clock like you had, we know it is interfering with their breathing."

One week later she and I were flying home. We made the trip unplanned but had no other choice. We had no appointment, found the spike, and got the small apartment, among many other events that fell into place. There again God had his hand over us the whole time.

Vonda now is an RN in the surgery department of a large hospital in

Indianapolis. I remember the first time she came home from work after they had performed a brain surgery. She was so excited to finally see what had been done to her.

Vonda and Londa

CHAPTER

10

Our Adult Lives

Don't walk in front of me,
I may not follow.
Don't walk behind me, I may not lead.
Just walk beside me and be my friend.

Albert Camus

Joan, Ed, Norie, Leon, Jim, Kat, Mil, and George

Today as we are growing older, with pride, we are still a close-knit family. We never have missed a Christmas Day as a family. As the years have gone by, our children always have known this was our day. We have a lot of picnics in the summertime and the kids always want to be sure George will be there to play with them. All of our children are very close, like we were when we were growing up. They have their own parties and game nights.

We get together at one another's homes for gospel sing-a-longs. Leon's wife, Betty, plays the guitar and we beg, borrow, or steal a piano player for the sing-a-longs. I took piano lessons for one year but then my teacher threw in the towel and moved. I never was the sharpest pencil in the tray when it came to music and I probably gave her a few gray hairs.

Many years passed as we all went our separate ways. Some were rockier than others and some daydreamed their way through the years.

If I could have had a choice in our life plan, I would have chosen the life we had over the lives of children today. We had no drugs, booze, peer pressure, and no lack of self-esteem. We were taught perseverance and patience, which I'm sure we did not always have. It taught us good work ethics, humor, and a deep love for God. Our lives were, and still are, truly an incredible journey. Our lives were like a puzzle, and once all the pieces locked into place, our lives made sense.

Each and every person in this book is a big part of our lives. We are best friends as well as family. We can count on each other when there is a crisis, and in a family this size, we have had a few. We learned the importance of making choices in life and then learned to accept the results of our choices. Whenever I think back to those days, I am amazed at what a love developed among so many people in a three-room house. We all are happily married, parents, successful, and have good lives. That's our payoff and reward.

Back: Norie, Kat, and George
Front: Leon, Jim, and Mil

Love means the same to all, regardless of color, age, or gender. To give love and to be loved is the greatest joy in the whole world. The six of us stayed married to our original spouses and always were able to say to our children, "I love you", something most of us never heard as children. All have settled in Indianapolis, within a thirty-mile radius of one another. This story may seem like it comes in eight different layers. That could be the case as we children learned to cope with the toils of life being loyal, cheerful, brave, reverent, clean, courteous, kind, and obedient.

Cousin Ed's life was anything but easy. When he was born, his father, also named Edward, told his mother, Emma, the baby died at birth and then sent Ed to be raised by his paternal grandmother. His father and Emma divorced soon after. Six months after Ed's birth, his father had another child, Hattie, by another woman, Juanita. They later married and had three more children together.

When Ed was old enough to ask questions about his mother, he was told Emma died during childbirth. Ed was thirty-nine years old when a family friend told him his mother was alive.

He searched for her and discovered she lived in Southbridge, Massachusetts. After finding out where she lived, he called her and made arrangements to visit with her. They spent two wonderful weeks together.

By that time she was sixty-four years old and had a bad heart. She died a short time after his visit.

While in Texas, Ed met and married a girl named Frances and they had one son. Ed tried out for the Houston Buff Baseball Team as a pitcher and made the team; however, he was newly married and Frances did not want him to travel with the team. She was too young to realize what an experience this could have been for both of them. Their marriage ended in divorce.

Ed returned to Indianapolis, and met and married Hazel. Their marriage lasted twenty-eight years and they had three sons. Ed worked for Stark and Wetzel Meat Packing House in Indianapolis for twenty-two years.

Ed and Hazel divorced and he returned to Texas, where he remarried Frances, thirty-one years after their divorce. They now live in Huffman, Texas, and make annual trips to Indianapolis to visit all of us.

Cousin John is married to May, his wife of fifty years, and they had four boys. May owned the only grocery store in Rye, Texas, for many years. John has been an over-the-road semi driver and mechanic all of his adult life and is active in HAM radios. John is still working and he and May live in Rye.

Cousin Hattie, after arriving in Houston with Aunt Mil, married very young. She had four children and died young in 1988.

Cousin Paul, who died at sixteen, always wanted to be a preacher. Well, I am sure he has been fulfilling his mission for many years by now.

Cousin Ella married young and had six children but divorced at an early age. She, too, lives in Rye, Texas.

Cousin Vic went to work for Omar Bakery where he met Mary Stephens. They were married in 1952, and have five children. Around 1979, Vic and Mary took his aging father George into their home where he stayed for two long, trying years before going to Joan's home. Vic has retired from various jobs and today he works at Duo Water Company owned by his son. Vic is still going strong at 68 years old.

Cousin Joan and Vic's mother Hazel wasn't around much in their lives. When Joan was young, Aunt Mil used to say to her, "You Hazel-looking thing, you!" Joan hated that statement for many years. After she was grown and had children of her own, Joan said she looked in the mirror and said, "Why shouldn't I look like her? She gave birth to me." This little talk with herself in the mirror was the turning point in her life.

Psalm 27:10 reads, "*When my father and mother forsake me, then the Lord will take me up.*" This is what happened to the lives of our many cousins.

Joan took her seventy-year-old father into her home around Labor Day, 1980, the weekend his sister, our Aunt Mil, died. George stayed with her until October 1984. Joan never called him Dad, but George. He hadn't really changed much but he was her father. She heard him in his room at night saying his prayers, just like a child.

On one occasion he asked her, with a twinkle in his eye, "Honey, will you take me over here to see this lady?" She answered, "Now George, I can't bear the idea of sharing you with another woman." He complained, "Well, I am cold," and she replied, "I will buy you a blanket." She went out the next day and bought him an electric blanket.

Even though he was very old and sick, he still loved the women and didn't want to give them up. George had a real thing for the ladies. Once Joan bought him some new clothes to go to the ballet and invited a lady she thought he would like to join them, to keep him happy. Joan did not know he already had met a lady at the senior citizens center and invited her. After they found their seats on the third floor, he kept finding excuses to go to the restroom or to get a drink or refreshments. She found out later that he had the other lady sitting on the first floor and was running up and down, keeping both women entertained.

Reflecting on how she felt her life turned out, Joan said, "What was meant for evil, God turned around and made something good of it." Her life. Even though George never apologized for abandoning her and her brother as teenagers, she said she loved him unconditionally, as Jesus taught us.

Joan has been married to Wesley Crum for many years. They have five children and own a cabinet business in Mount Vernon, Ohio.

Our Family ~ 2001

Back: Shelly, Gary, Phyllis, Bob, Vonda, Steve, Barb, Chet, Danny, Donna, Paul
Middle: Leon, Nate, Damien (baby), George, Norie, Jim, Janet, Bev, Mil, Kat, Marsha
Front: Christie, Londa, Steve Jr., Curtis

CHAPTER

11

Our Family Servicemen

John 15:13

*Greater love hath no man than this, that a
man lay down his life for his friends.*

Chapter 11

At a memorial service for World War II veterans in October, 2002, Senator Bill Harris, 19th District, State of Ohio, had the following to say:

"I would like to extend my most heartfelt gratitude to all of you; my respect and esteem for every one of you goes beyond words. To knowingly and willingly put your life in danger for a noble cause in representation of your country is one of the greatest things a man can do in his life. It takes bravery, unselfishness, and love for what is good and right to do what you did. War is a terrible thing; only the men who have gone through it and witnessed it can truly comprehend the horrors of war. Yet without brave men such as yourselves, the powers of evil would have conquered us all many years ago.

"Once a man goes through a war, he realizes what it means to be brave. A man isn't brave when he does great things without any fear; a man is brave when he does great things despite his fear. The greater the fear, the braver the man who overcomes it and still does what is required of him. That is the difference between a hero and a coward. Both of them feel fear, but when the coward turns back, the hero continues on. I would like to thank all of you for quelling your fears and standing up for what is right. You are all heroes."

August Victor Wood
(father)

WWI, enlisted in 1918; trained at Naval Training Station in Great Lakes, Illinois; started as an Apprentice Seaman. He was a Fireman 3rd Class when discharged.

Edward F. Wood, Sr.
(brother of August)

WWI, 1917-1918, U.S. Army

George E. Wood
(brother of August)

WWII; trained Fort Lewis, Washington, for one year; sailed from Boston, Massachusetts, on the

Miles Standish ship in 1944, in -30° weather; stationed at Aubry Hall, Nuneaton, Warwickshire, England, 737th Tank Battalion.

George received two Bronze Stars and a Good Conduct Medal. Patton's Spearheaders 737th participated in all five major battles--Normandy, Northern France, Ardennes-Alsace, Rhineland, and Central Europe. During 299 days of actual combat, members of the unit were awarded two Distinguished Service Crosses, 22 Silver Stars, 188 Bronze Stars, more than 400 Purple Hearts, and two Croix de Guerre's. Three enlisted men received battlefield commissions.

The unit landed at Omaha Beach on July 12th and 13th, 1944, assigned to the First Army after the capture of Saint Lo in France. The 737th was transferred to the Third Army on August 6, 1944. Although it fought most of the war with the Third Army, the battalion was loaned briefly to the First Army again in 1945, to help clean up the Ruhr Pocket that contained 317,000 German soldiers. This campaign started at Brilon and ended in Menden on the Ruhr River. In five days, the 737th cleared 42 towns. One of the reconnaissance patrols killed

Lieutenant General Joachim Von Kortzfleisch, second in command to Field Marshal Walter Model, when he tried to escape.

At times the battalion was badly mauled by some of the best soldiers in the German army. The Germans destroyed 66 medium and 8 light tanks. (A tank battalion has an initial strength of 59 medium tanks, 17 light tanks, and 751 men.)

Combat took a heavy toll in manpower. The unit had 6 officers and 58 enlisted men killed in action. One officer and 20 enlisted men were reported missing. The names of one officer and two enlisted men are listed on the wall in the Luxembourg Cemetery as soldiers "who sleep in unknown graves."

Those losses were not without glory. When General Patton was observing our troops at the Moselle River crossing, he said, "That's the way tanks should fight."

General Patton sent a letter on November 17, 1945, to the officers and men of the 5th Infantry Division, to whom the 737th was attached. He wrote:

"To my mind, history does not record incidents of greater valor than your assault crossings of the Sauer and the

Rhine. You crossed so many rivers I am persuaded many of you have web feet..."

Another historical incident occurred in Volary--the last official casualty in the ETO. A Czech-American citizen, Pfc. Charles Havlat of the 803rd Tank Destroyer Battalion, was killed when elements of the 11th Panzer Division ambushed his reconnaissance platoon four kilometers northeast of the town. This event took place at 0820 hours on May 7, ten minutes before the "cease-fire" orders became effective.

George E. Wood
(brother)

Drafted into the U.S. Army in January 1953, during the Korean War. George was first cook. When he was discharged in October 1954, he was a 1st Sergeant.

In George's division at the children's home he met and became friends with Bill Walker. They played sports together and went to school together and became best friends, but after leaving the home, they went their separate ways. When George came home from the army he found out his lifelong friend had terminal cancer.

Gary L. Wood (George's son)

Enlisted 1984-1990 as electronics technician. Gary was stationed for four years on the U.S.S. Nassau out of Norfolk, which was an LHA-4, Landing and Helicopter Assault craft. He maintained and repaired ship communications equipment.

James Milton Wood (brother)

Jim spent two years in Germany as a clerk typist in the Army and worked for the motor pool department. He was in an automobile accident in Germany and spent eight weeks in the hospital.

Chapter 11

Leon D. Wood
(brother)

Enlisted in the U.S. Navy 1952-1954. Leon sailed on the U.S.S. Los Angeles. In 1954, he was a first gunner mate and had duties in the Philippines and Hawaii.

Once they were sailing under the Golden Gate Bridge. When ships are on the waters, the Navy always has the right of way. Another ship was heading towards them with no intention of yielding and the U.S.S. Los Angeles' captain was worried, to say the least. After all was said and done, the captain said he could not have gotten his finger between the two ships. This was a good reason for all on the ship to have great concern.

John Steven Wood
(cousin)

Served in the Air Force 1954-1960. John spent 19 months in the Philippines and two years in Germany. He was an instructor in the ground power equipment mechanics division.

☆   ☆   ☆

Edward Frank Wood
(cousin)

Enlisted 1949. He was an instructor in the Army Alaskan Ski Troopers and he taught survival in the wilderness.

☆   ☆   ☆

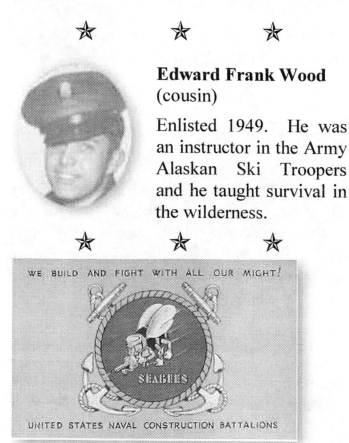

Frank Tooley, Jr.
(cousin)

WWII, U.S. Naval Seabee, Construction Battalion

Chapter 11

Chester A. Chase
(Mil's husband)

Drafted into the Army in December 1951, with basic training at Camp Chaffee, Arkansas. He was shipped to Pusan, Korea, trucked north past Seoul, to the 69th Field Artillery, Charlie Company of the 25th Infantry Division, supporting artillery fire for the 14th Infantry Regiment, where his brother Phillip was a BAR rifle sniper. Phillip enlisted at 18 years of age and was shipped directly to Korea in 1952.

Chester arrived at the front lines in January 1953. In March, he flew to Japan for two weeks of intensive training in chemical, biological, and radiological warfare. They had firefights every night and most days around the hills the men called "Old Baldy", "White Horse", "Jane Russell", and others.

When the 14th Regiment pulled back for R&R, the 69th moved over to Kumsong sector manned by the 1st Rock Capital Division of the South Korean Army.

Multiple divisions of the North Korean Army attacked the South Koreans during the spring monsoons. The 69th set up in fortified bunkers in a valley. After three days and nights of intense artillery firing with incoming mortar and artillery fire, the South Korean infantry was overrun to where the 69th was. The 555th Artillery Battalion flanking the 69th was taken prisoner of war. Thanks to their captain, a WWII officer, the 69th got out with minimum casualties. Chester was hit by small pieces of mortar shrapnel but kept moving.

The 69th had to demolish their own bunkers and ammunition before pulling back and digging in on the mountain. Along with the infantries, they attacked the North Koreans with intense artillery fire, mortar, and small arms fire for four days and nights without rest. The unit received commendations from the division general for firing 1,030 Howitzer rounds in three days.

The North Koreans always were drugged and had only rice to eat when on the offensive. Following several more skirmishes into the summer, a cease-fire was arranged, and they dug in to hold the 38th Parallel line of resistance.

Later Chester rotated back to the States on a ship through a Pacific typhoon to San Francisco, and then on to Des Moines with three aircraft engine failures, and was discharged at Chicago on January 25, 1954. To this day, Chester refuses to fly!

Bill R. Brodie
(Kat's husband)

WWII; enlisted July, 1941, to December, 1945, in the Army Air Force as an airplane and engine mechanic. Bill performed first and second echelon maintenance and repair on C-47's and C-60's. He was in charge of a fleet of 14 airplanes and supervised the work of 40 men. He served as flight engineer on C-47 for eight months.

Ohio Senate
Senate Building
Columbus, Ohio 43215
614-466-8086
bharris@maild.sen.state.oh.us

Committees:
Reference, Chairman
Education, Vice Chair
Finance and Financial Institutions
Economic Development
    Technology & Aerospace
Agriculture
Rules

Controlling Board
Joint Legislative Ethics Committee
Ohio School Facilities Commission
Legislative Committee
    on Education Oversight
Ohio War Orphans
    Scholarship Board

Senator Bill M. Harris
19th District

October 9, 2002

Dear Esteemed Sirs,

I would like to extend my most heartfelt gratitude to all of you; my respect and esteem for everyone of you goes beyond words. To knowingly and willingly put you life in danger for a noble cause in representation of your country is one of the greatest things a man can do in his life. It takes bravery, unselfishness, and a love for what is good and right to do what you did. War is a terrible thing, only the men who have gone through it and witnessed it can truly comprehend the horrors of war. Yet, without brave men such as yourselves, the powers of evil would have conquered us all many years ago.

Once a man goes through a war, he realizes what it means to be brave. A man isn't brave when he does great things without any fear; a man is brave when he does great things despite his fear. The greater the fear, the braver the man who overcomes it and still does what is required of him. That is the difference between a hero, and a coward. Both of them feel fear, but when the coward turns back, the hero continues on. I would like to thank all of you for quelling your fears and standing up to for what is right. You are all heroes.

Sincerely,

Bill Harris

Bill Harris
State Senator
19th Senate District

Letter from Senator Harris

The Wood Family Tree

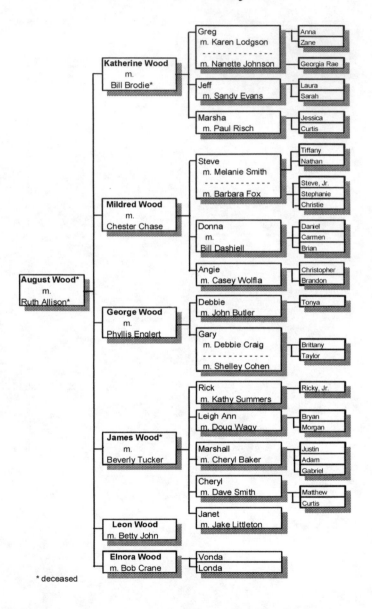

* deceased

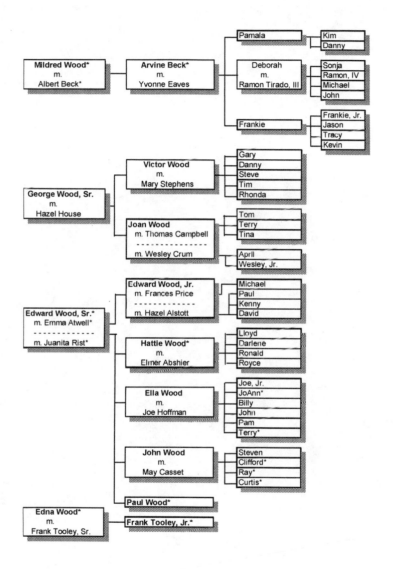

Mildred Wood*
m.
Albert Beck*

Arvine Beck*
m.
Yvonne Eaves

Pamala
- Kim
- Danny

Deborah
m.
Ramon Tirado, III
- Sonja
- Ramon, IV
- Michael
- John

Frankie
- Frankie, Jr.
- Jason
- Tracy
- Kevin

George Wood, Sr.
m.
Hazel House

Victor Wood
m.
Mary Stephens
- Gary
- Danny
- Steve
- Tim
- Rhonda

Joan Wood
m. Thomas Campbell
- - - - - - - - - - - - - - - -
m. Wesley Crum
- Tom
- Terry
- Tina
- April
- Wesley, Jr.

Edward Wood, Sr.*
m. Emma Atwell*
- - - - - - - - - - - - -
m. Juanita Rist*

Edward Wood, Jr.
m. Frances Price
- - - - - - - - - - - - - -
m. Hazel Alstott
- Michael
- Paul
- Kenny
- David

Hattie Wood*
m.
Elmer Abshier
- Lloyd
- Darlene
- Ronald
- Royce

Ella Wood
m.
Joe Hoffman
- Joe, Jr.
- JoAnn*
- Billy
- John
- Pam
- Terry*

John Wood
m.
May Casset
- Steven
- Clifford*
- Ray*
- Curtis*

Paul Wood*

Edna Wood*
m.
Frank Tooley, Sr.

Frank Tooley, Jr.*

Epilogue

God certainly held the Wood Family in the palm of His hand. Here are the meanings of many of our names.

- August Victor ~ exalted
- Katherine (Kat) ~ pure
- Mildred (Mil) ~ gentle spirit
- James (Jim) ~ nurtured
- George ~ walks with God
- Leon ~ brave as a lion
- Elnora (Norie) ~ bright as the sun
- John ~ God is gracious
- Edward (Ed) ~ guardian of happiness
- Hattie ~ ruler of the household
- Paul ~ dynamo of energy and faith
- Ella ~ kindred spirit
- Joan ~ God is gracious
- Victor ~ triumphant spirit
- Mildred (Aunt Mil) Beck ~ gentle spirit
- Albert Beck ~ brilliant
- Arvine Beck ~ gracious son

ABOUT THE AUTHOR

This is Elnora Wood Crane's first book. She wrote the book primarily as a gift to her growing, extended family, but also it is her hope that all who read it will be inspired not to give up on life and love, even though the roads in life are rough. She often calls to mind the saying "It's in the valleys that we grow."

Elnora has been married thirty-eight happy years to her husband Bob, and they have two grown daughters. They reside in Indianapolis, Indiana.